# The Role of the Pension Fund Trustee

# The Role of the Pension Fund Trustee

## John Cunliffe

Partner, McKenna & Co, Solicitors

In association with the National Association of Pension Funds

Croner Publications Ltd
Croner House
London Road
Kingston upon Thames
Surrey KT2 6SR
Tel: 081-547 3333

Copyright © J.Cunliffe
First published 1989
Second edition 1991

Published by
Croner Publications Ltd
Croner House
London Road
Kingston upon Thames
Surrey KT2 6SR
Telephone: 081–547 3333

The right of John Cunliffe to be identified as author of this work has
been asserted by him in accordance with the Copyright, Designs and Patents Act 1988.

While every care has been taken
in the writing and editing of this book,
readers should be aware that only Acts of Parliament
and Statutory Instruments have the force of law,
and that only the courts can authoritatively
interpret the law.

British Library Cataloguing in Publication Data
Cunliffe, John
The role of the pension fund trustee
1. Great Britain. Superannuation schemes. Trusteeship
I. Title
658.3′253

ISBN 1-85524-091-2

Printed in Great Britain by
Whitstable Litho Printers Ltd., Whitstable, Kent.

# CONTENTS

Preface to the First Edition                                           vii
Preface to the Second Edition                                           ix
Foreword                                                                xi
Chapter 1    What is a Trust?                                            1
Chapter 2    Creation of Trusts                                         3
Chapter 3    Appointment and Removal of Trustees                        5
Chapter 4    Duties of Trustees                                        13
Chapter 5    The Trustees' Discretionary Powers                        17
Chapter 6    Investment Powers                                         33
Chapter 7    The Financial Services Act 1986                           43
Chapter 8    Disclosure                                                53
Chapter 9    Accounts and Trustees' Reports                            61
Chapter 10   Delegation, Conflict and Disagreement                     73
Chapter 11   Merger and Winding Up                                     81
Chapter 12   The Liability of Trustees                                 89
Chapter 13   Equal Treatment                                          91
Chapter 14   Taxation and Revenue Limits                             103
Chapter 15   Surpluses                                               113
Chapter 16   An Outline of State Pensions, Occupational
             Pensions and Personal Pensions                          121
Chapter 17   Contracting Out                                         129
Chapter 18   Preservation                                            133
Chapter 19   Transfers                                               135
Chapter 20   Help for the Individual                                 143
Chapter 21   Increases to Pensions in Payment                        151
Chapter 22   Who owns a Pension Scheme's Surplus?                    159
Chapter 23   Principles of Trusteeship                               169
Chapter 24   Glossary of Terms                                       171
Index                                                                179

# PREFACE TO THE FIRST EDITION

This book developed out of the Pension Fundamentals Course run by the National Association of Pension Funds. Angela Smith, the Council Member responsible for Pension Fundamentals, took a risk when she launched me on to 80 unsuspecting trainee pension administrators in September 1987. I have much to thank both her and them for. If they learned half as much as me, they will be fortunate. Some of the material in the book, including the Lawyer's Tales, appeared first in the pages of *Pensions Management*. My thanks are due to *Pensions Management* for so freely agreeing to their reproduction and to the three editors, for whom I have written, for so generously indulging my eccentricities.

It would also be ungenerous as well as ungracious for me not to thank —

my wife who has suffered (her word) long absences from my company while the book was being written;

my friends Andrew Bayliss and Keith Boughton for tolerating with good humour their portrayal as young David and John Watson in the Lawyer's Tales;

Colin Bamford for teaching me that pensions people are more important than lawyers and that actuaries are the most important of all;

McKenna & Co, and especially the hard pressed members of the Employment and Pensions Department, for allowing me to spend some of my time on writing and speaking, when they might well have thought that I should have stuck my nose more firmly to the grindstone;

the National Association of Pension Funds for sponsoring the book and taking endless time and trouble over it;

last and not least to Sheila Carpenter for reducing chaos to order and providing an acceptable face for my manuscript.

John Cunliffe
May 1989

# PREFACE TO THE SECOND EDITION

It is two years since this book first appeared. As all the existing stocks have now been sold, a new edition is needed. In any event the passage of the Social Security Act 1990 in response to the Occupational Pensions Board's report *Protecting Pensions* necessitated a large number of changes. Furthermore, the decision of the European Court of Justice in *Barber v Guardian Royal Exchange* meant that the chapter on equal treatment had to be completely rewritten. The second edition takes full account of all these changes and has, as well as the chapter on equal treatment, new chapters on help for the individual, increases to pensions in payment and on ownership of surplus. They reflect a period of rapid change and increasing interest in the field of pensions.

First time readers of "The Lawyer's Tales", which illustrate the text of the book, may be a little baffled because they are not arranged in chronological order, but in order of subject. Readers need to know that it is not only the law that has changed. Archie Smithers and young David — the heroes, if that is the right word, of the Tales — effected a management buyout of the Magnificent Mutual Assurance Society's documents department. The buyout, under the name of Docs Galore, has gone from strength to strength. It should not be necessary to mention that neither the Magnificent Mutual nor Archie Smithers and David really exist. Although Archie is loosely based on myself and David on Andrew Bayliss, in reality the two characters would be completely unemployable; hopefully Andrew and I are not.

The law in this book is based on the law of England and Wales in force at the time of going to press. However in the case of some of the references to disclosure of information, trustees' reports and self-investment, it is based on draft regulations which may be subject to change.

Finally, in addition to those whom I thanked in the last edition, I would like to take this opportunity of thanking:

- my fellow partner in the Employee Benefits Group at McKennas
  — Simon Jeffreys — who is a greater source of guidance and strength than he realises;

- my colleague Mark Kowalik who bears the heat of the day when Archie is away at conferences and David is playing cricket (in fact this book was his idea);
- my friend and erstwhile colleague Steve Mingle who bears a passing resemblance to the Magnificent Mutual's deputy pensions actuary;
- my friend Colin Steward at the NAPF for taking the trouble to read the book in typescript and for his patient help and guidance; and
- not least my secretary Donna Waters whose working life alternates between furious activity when Archie and David are actually working and relative idleness during their frequent absences.

June 1991
John Cunliffe

# FOREWORD

I am very pleased to be asked to write the "Foreword" to this new edition of "The Role of the Pension Fund Trustee". When the book was originally published in 1989 it was welcomed by my predecessor as an up-to-date guide for pension scheme trustees which embraced recent developments. This new edition will ensure that it remains topical.

Recent years have seen sweeping changes in pensions and these are not finished yet. The radical changes introduced by United Kingdom legislation, and the increasing intrusion of EC law into pension matters, combine to make the role of the trustee more complicated than ever. United Kingdom legislation has often taken the form of enabling legislation to be enforced by regulations and it is not unusual for there to be a considerable period of time between enactment, and the coming into force of the appropriate regulations. The trustee needs to be able to rely on expert guidance to fulfil his or her duties with confidence.

The added consumer protection provided by the Pensions Ombudsman, who started to take cases in April 1991, will result in the actions of trustees coming under even greater scrutiny than before. More than ever trustees will need to give careful consideration to all the available facts, and ensure that they are aware of the current provisions of scheme trust deeds and rules as well as any relevant over-riding legislation, whether in the United Kingdom or the EC, before reaching a decision. Records will need to be carefully kept, in many cases for long years, so that any decision can be supported by the relevant papers.

"The Role of the Pension Fund Trustee" is not a weighty legal text. Rather it is intended as a straightforward guide to help trustees understand their role, the nature of their duties and the implications of recent developments so that they can act in a more effective manner.

The book also represents a practical demonstration of the commitment to providing information and training for trustees to which the NAPF is dedicated. Much of John Cunliffe's thinking about the book was stimulated by his contribution to NAPF courses. In addition to its general information role, the book will be an important adjunct to a number of the courses run by the Association.

The National Association of Pension Funds is, therefore, pleased to be associated with the publication of this latest edition of "The Role of the Pension Fund Trustee", which it sees as an integral part of the services provided to its members.

Brian MacMahon
Chairman
National Association
of Pension Funds
June 1989

# CHAPTER 1

# What is a Trust?

## Definition of a trust

A trust is simply an arrangement under which one person or group of people called trustees hold property — the assets of the trust — for the benefit of others, called beneficiaries. Trustees are so called because they are trusted by the person who sets up the trust to administer the trust assets, not for their own benefit, but for the benefit of the beneficiaries. An occupational pension scheme is a good example of a trust. The trustees hold the assets for the benefit of the members and pensioners. Another example is a village hall where the people in the village have the right to use the hall in accordance with its rules. The legal title to the hall is vested in the trustees who administer it, pay the caretaker and allow people to use it in accordance with the rules.

## Contract and trust

A personal pension is a half-way house. An individual enters into a contract with a pension provider that, in return for the payment of the contributions, the provider will pay a pension to the individual at a selected age. But the provider must also enter into enforceable obligations to third parties. Thus any widow, widower or other person who becomes entitled to any payment under the scheme, which gives effect to protected rights, must be able to enforce that entitlement. A trust is one method of achieving this. A contract creates personal rights which cannot be enforced by anyone who is not a party to it. A trust creates rights which are enforceable by third parties and does not, unlike a contract, require the person enforcing the rights to give consideration or something in return. Accordingly a pension scheme which is set up as a trust can be enforced by members who were not even alive when it was

# Reasons for a trust

There are however two other reasons for a trust. The first is that the assets of the trust are separated from the employer's property. This is so even if the employer is the sole trustee of the pension scheme. He or she will hold the scheme assets in a separate legal capacity. They are therefore not available to the employer's creditors. And so if the employer goes into liquidation, the liquidator cannot claim the pension scheme's assets for the benefit of creditors. This legal separation of the pension scheme assets is a valuable protection to the members whose accrued benefits are, at least to the extent of the assets, secured. It also means that the assets are invested to produce a return for the scheme. The alternative would be for the contributions to be used by the employer in the business and pensions simply paid out of revenue when they become due. This would deprive the members of the independent security of an asset backing for their benefits.

# Inland Revenue requirements

The second reason for having a trust is that it is a condition of Inland Revenue approval. If a pension scheme is set up under irrevocable trusts and various other conditions are satisfied, the Inland Revenue will approve it. This means that various valuable tax breaks are given. An employee's contributions are tax deductible. Not only are the employer's contributions allowed as a trading expense, they are not taxable as a benefit in kind in the employee's hands. The investment income and capital gains of the scheme are exempt from tax. The pensions ultimately payable are taxed as earned income and a tax free cash sum can be paid to the member on retirement, and to his or her dependants on his or her death in service. It is the giving of tax approval that confers these advantages.

# CHAPTER 2

# Creation of Trusts

## How a trust is established

Except where land is concerned, there are no formalities needed to establish a trust. It can be done by word of mouth. In the case of land a written document is necessary. But in practice trusts are always created by a written document. Imagine the problems if you tried to set up a pension scheme by word of mouth. Who would remember all the details and for how long?

## Signed and delivered

For that good practical reason, therefore, the trusts of a pension scheme are written down. A deed is not legally required but is almost invariably used. This means that instead of simply signing the document, a person signs and delivers it. Signing needs no explanation. Delivering the deed means that the person concerned intends to be legally bound by it and delivers or hands over the document to someone else as proof of this.

Pension schemes are sometimes set up by resolution of a company's board of directors. A number of personal pension schemes were established in this way. Occupational pension schemes, however, are usually set up by a deed. Two kinds of document are used for this purpose — an interim trust deed and a definitive trust deed and rules. What is the difference between them?

## Interim deeds

An interim trust deed is a document that is used to get a pension scheme going in a short time span. It is a short deed containing basic trust established. Thus one of the reasons for using a trust to set up a pension scheme is to enable the beneficiaries to enforce their rights.

provisions relating, for example, to contracting-out, if appropriate, transfers in and out, investment, appointment and removal of trustees and winding up. Attached to it will be an announcement or booklet setting out the essential features of the scheme such as contributions and benefits. This procedure enables the scheme to be established with a minimum of delay. The Inland Revenue will not grant the scheme full tax approval before the definitive trust deed and rules, which set out the constitution of the scheme in full, is entered into. But the Revenue will grant provisional relief from tax on employees' contributions and will not charge to tax as benefits in kind the employer's contributions.

## Definitive trust deed and rules

A definitive trust deed and rules then has to be prepared within a two year period, which can be extended with the Revenue's consent. This is a lengthy document which contains full details of all the scheme benefits, company and members' contributions, all the provisions required by legislation relating to preservation, Inland Revenue limits on maximum benefits, contracting-out and the like. Essentially, pension schemes can be very simple, but successive waves of legislation relating to early leavers, compulsory transfer rights, revaluation of preserved benefits and contracting-out have made the drafting of definitive trust deeds and rules a complex job. The document has to be read and approved, with or without amendments, by both the employer and the trustees. It then has to be approved by the Superannuation Funds Office of the Inland Revenue and the Occupational Pensions Board before full tax approval is granted, resulting in exemption from income and capital gains tax on the investments of the scheme. It is a long process and often takes the two years allotted for the task. In practice it would usually be impossible to set up a pension scheme from scratch using a definitive trust deed and rules; it would simply take too long.

# CHAPTER 3

# Appointment and Removal of Trustees

## First trustees

The first trustees of the scheme are appointed by the interim trust deed. This deed will also usually give the employer power to remove the trustees and appoint others in their place. There is no upper or lower limit on the number of trustees and the employer can be either the only trustee or one of the trustees of the scheme. However, the trust deed often specifies a maximum and minimum number of trustees. The practice of having the employer as the sole trustee of the scheme causes conflicts of interest and, although not unlawful, it is not favoured by the Occupational Pensions Board.

## Statutory provisions

If the trust deed does not deal with the appointment and removal of trustees, the matter is regulated by the Trustee Act 1925. That gives the power to appoint trustees to the person, if any, nominated in the trust deed; in the absence of such a power the trustees are given the power to appoint new trustees. There is no power given by the Trustee Act to remove a trustee and so this power has to be given in the trust deed.

## Resignation of trustees

A trustee cannot simply resign or retire. Either a new trustee has to be appointed in his place or at least two individual trustees or a corporate trustee (a trust corporation) must remain in office and give their consent. Because this can be a nuisance, scheme rules usually confer a power of removal on the employer. This gets over the difficulty which arises when a trustee, who is an employee of the company, gives in his or her notice and resigns as a trustee. Alternatively the employee may assume that, having left, he or she is no longer a trustee. This is not the case and a properly worded power of appointment and removal in the rules will avoid these problems.

## Types of trustee

There are various types of trustee. First there are individual trustees who may or may not be employees of the company concerned. Individual trustees need no further explanation. They will be reimbursed their expenses but are not usually paid for their services. Then there are corporate trustees. Here a company is appointed as the sole trustee or one of the trustees. Such a company is usually a subsidiary of or controlled by the principal employer. Its directors will take the place of individual trustees. This is a change of form rather than substance but does avoid the need for numerous deeds of removal and appointment when the individuals cease to hold office. If they are individual trustees, usually a deed will be needed; this is not the case if they are directors of a corporate trustee, who can be changed by a board resolution.

## Trust corporations

A trust corporation is a particular kind of corporate trustee, usually a bank or an insurance company with experience of managing large trusts and pension schemes. A trust corporation has to have an issued share capital of £250,000 of which not less than £100,000 is paid up. Such a corporation can act as sole trustee where otherwise the scheme might need two individuals. A trust corporation will require to be paid for its services.

## Custodian trustees

A custodian trustee is simply a trustee appointed to have safe custody of the scheme's assets, for example share certificates and the like. A custodian trustee acts on the instructions of the ordinary trustees, who are then in this situation often called managing trustees. Custodian trustees have rather gone out of favour. They cause duplication of records, need to be paid and can only be got rid of by applying to the court for a removal order.

## Pensioneer trustees

Pensioneer trustees are special trustees approved by the Inland Revenue. Certain small pension schemes have to have a pensioneer trustee as one of the trustees. This is to ensure that the tax breaks given to approved schemes are not abused. A self administered pension scheme — as opposed to an insured scheme — with less than 12 members will normally, as a condition of Revenue approval, be required to have a pensioneer trustee. A pensioneer trustee is an individual or company widely involved with occupational pension schemes and having dealings with the Superannuation Funds Office who is prepared to undertake not to consent to an improper termination of the scheme. The Inland Revenue is currently reviewing its practice relating to small schemes, and, as a result, the pensioneer trustee may become, in effect, a watchdog for the Inland Revenue, and be required to report any improper dealings involving the scheme.

## Independent trustees

On an employer's insolvency an independent trustee has to be appointed to protect the members' interests. There are other occasions, for example a threatened takeover of the employer, where it is often found desirable to have independent trustees, who are not constrained by pressure from the old or new employer. Independent trustees are dealt with in Chapter 20 "Help for the Individual".

For an illustration of some of the problems that can arise with the appointment and removal of trustees readers are referred to "The Lawyer's Tale: Poison Pills", which follows this chapter.

# The Lawyer's Tale: Poison Pills

Maud Blenkinsop was the daughter in J. Blenkinsop and Daughter, Ironfounders Ltd, established by her family a century ago in the Isle of Dogs. Nowadays they made widgets. Like many another British company they made a fair living but not nearly as much as if they had sold their valuable freehold to be developed for yuppy housing and invested the proceeds in gilt-edged securities. Maud, who had run the company since her father's death, was a handsome woman in her early 60s. In her youth it was said that she had been beautiful, but she had never married. She devoted herself to the family business and was inclined to be headstrong and imperious.

Blenkinsops had had a company pension scheme for many years which the Magnificent Mutual Life Assurance Society looked after. As a result of the recession in the widget trade and a buoyant stock market, the pension scheme had built up a large surplus; the pension fund was in fact worth more than the company.

Roger Davenport was the pensions superintendent assigned by the Magnificent Mutual to look after the scheme. He was the youngest ever superintendent appointed by old Murgatroyd, the Chief General Manager. He was not quite 30, was tall, had blond curly hair and was thought by the girls in his section to be devastatingly good looking. He dressed conservatively in a dark grey suit and white shirt. His one sartorial lapse was a teenage tendency to wear white socks and black suede shoes. More to the point, he was an Associate of the Institute of Pensions Management. He was good at his job and it was considered a great prize to be asked to work on his team. This consisted of six girls who clucked like contented hens at their desks all day.

He was a great favourite of Maud Blenkinsop who, not being unsusceptible to masculine charm, invited Roger to visit her to discuss the pension scheme rather more often than was strictly necessary. The triennial actuarial valuation had recently been prepared and Roger had arranged a meeting with Maud to discuss this.

Roger expected that Maud would wish to use the surplus to make a repayment to the company (which could have done with the money) or to have a contribution holiday. He was surprised, therefore, when Maud explained that instead she wanted the money used to improve the benefits and to make the scheme secure against raiders.

"The writing is on the wall for Blenkinsops," she said. "We don't make as much profit now as we did 10 years ago; we have this valuable freehold ripe for development, and we have a pension scheme worth more than the company."

She may have had a penchant for handsome young men, but she was no fool. Maud then explained that she owned 25% of the company's shares but the other three quarters were held by her two nephews who were both accountants in the City. "I expect you know the type," she said. "They probably worry for an hour before deciding it is safe to cross the road. They are overpaid and insensitive - you cannot imagine how dreary they are."

"Oh, but I can," cut in Roger. "You should meet our actuaries. They make your nephews sound positively exciting."

"Well," continued Maud, "I know that sooner or later we will get a good offer for the company and my dearest nephews will sell us all up lock, stock and barrel and put me out on the kerb. What I want to do is to safeguard the pension scheme and make sure that the pensions are safe. I hear that there are types in the City who buy up companies like this, strip out the surplus in the pension scheme and admit all their own employees into it. I believe it is called 'doing a quick strip'," she said looking a little longingly at Roger, who started to go red. "You must be able to do something to stop this sort of thing."

"I will ask our lawyer," said Roger, "and arrange a meeting next week."

The following week Roger and Archie Smithers, the Magnificent Mutual's lawyer, arrived at Maud's office. Archie explained that in essence what was required was to divert the key elements of control from the company to the trustees. Basically these were over the level of company funding, the appointment and removal of trustees, increases in pensions and what happened on the winding up of the scheme.

Usually the company paid the balance of the cost of funding the benefits after allowing for the members' contributions. The level of the company's contribution was, however, fairly flexible and it could be reduced, suspended or even terminated. If the company's obligation was fixed and there was no right to reduce or terminate it, this would obviously benefit the members. The problem is that it could be argued that to do this would not be in the company's interests and so beyond the powers of the directors.

At this point Maud said, a trifle irritably, "what is the point of putting up solutions if you immediately knock them down again?".

"Well," said Smithers, "I think it is important that you understand all the pros and cons. The second method of 'predator proofing' as it is sometimes called," he continued quickly, "relates to the power of appointing and removing trustees. Normally the trustees, who actually run the scheme, are appointed and can be removed by the company. This, of course, makes them to some extent lackeys of the employer because if they do or even threaten to do something which the employer does not want, they can be removed. Indeed, on a takeover one would expect the trustees to be removed and replaced by appointees of the new company."

"There is a point that you are leading up to, I suppose," intervened Maud impatiently. "Roger always gets through the business much more quickly and then we have a nice drink together."

"I am sorry," said Smithers — he knew the importance of the Blenkinsop scheme — "but I am afraid that this is a complicated subject. It is not something that can be run through in half an hour like routine pensions administration," he said with a barbed look at Roger. "If you change this so that the trustees cannot be appointed or removed by the company, but only by themselves, you remove a significant area of control from the company," Smithers continued. "The trustees can then run the scheme without interference from the company. Of course if they are employees as well as trustees, then their jobs will be on the line if they move out of step."

"Let me deal next with pension increases," Smithers continued. "I see from the actuarial report that you have increased pensions by 5% for each of the last three years. These increases were discretionary and were made by the trustees with the company's approval. But the company need not have given this and the trustees need not have awarded the increases. To get over this you can change the rules to give automatic pension increases every year, index-linked with a ceiling of, say, 5%. The pensioners would then be protected and the cost of this would by itself considerably eat into your surplus."

"You really do go on about things," sighed Maud impatiently. "I did want to have a quiet chat with Roger about one or two things. I had no idea we were going to endure such a rigmarole. We had all better have a drink. It might speed you up, Mr Smithers, but it will in any event make your words go down a bit better." She thereupon poured out, without asking Smithers or Roger if they wanted it, three enormous neat scotches. Having downed the first "half pint" from her glass she smiled graciously and said :

"Do continue, Mr Smithers, but please bear in mind that I have booked a table for lunch in half an hour."

Smithers managed to avoid getting flustered but was surprisingly jealous of his young colleague's cool in the face of this monstrous harridan.

"I have really only two more points," he said. "The first is that when a pension scheme is wound up, the rules lay down the order of priorities. When you have provided for pensions being paid and for members' accrued rights to benefit, the surplus is then allocated usually to augment members' benefits up to Inland Revenue limits with any balance being returned to the employer. The augmentation, as it is called, is usually carried out by the trustees with the employer's consent. To protect the members against an asset stripper, the rule would have to be changed to make the trustees increase the benefits — they would have no choice nor would they need the employer's consent.

"Secondly, the scheme could be closed to new members. It would not be possible therefore for a new company to admit its employees to the scheme and share in the surplus. I would recommend that this be done."

"Right then," said Maud, "you had better draw up a deed to make these changes. Have it done immediately and we will meet next week to sign it."

"I am afraid that it is not as simple as that," said Smithers silkily.

"What difficulties are you introducing now?" said Maud in tones of icy hauteur; Roger's suede shoes began to twitch in nervous sympathy.

"I can be very brief," said Smithers, "but I would be failing in my duty if I did not advise you about whether the predator proofing should be automatic or only triggered in the event of a takeover. There are difficulties about a triggered change. Some lawyers have argued that it is not within the company's powers to do this. If Blenkinsops was a public company and a takeover was imminent, you would need the consent of the Takeover Panel; but it is not a public company, and as a takeover seems inevitable, it is perhaps better to grasp the nettle and make the changes automatic. I will produce deeds drafted on the two alternative bases and you may care to discuss this with Roger."

With that Smithers withdrew and left Maud and Roger to their lunch. Later in the day the two colleagues met.

"I don't know how you put up with that formidable battleaxe," expostulated Archie. "You must have the patience of a saint. I am afraid that I am on holiday next week but David, my assistant, could come along to the meeting with the documents."

David and Roger presented themselves to Maud the following week. Maud's eyes lit up when she saw David who was a clean cut young man of 23. He explained the significance of the two alternative deeds and that Maud would have to live with the consequences if she chose the deed with the automatic changes. A triggering change could cause difficulties and might operate in the event of a reorganisation or a friendly takeover. On balance, it seemed best to have an out-and-out change of control and learn to live with it.

"My goodness," said Maud, "you are a young man of parts. You are beginning to compare very favourably with Roger, let alone that garrulous old goat, Smithers."

"There is just one last thing," gasped David with a red face. "Archie Smithers recommended closing the scheme to new entrants. He and I have talked about this further. The judge in the Hanson Trust case said that, while this could be done, it could not prevent the company and the trustees agreeing to re-open the scheme later on. We have nevertheless put it in our deeds because the trustees would have to agree to the scheme being re-opened and this should protect the members."

# The moral of this tale

The moral is that successful predator proofing is not a question of just knocking up a quick deed of amendment. It really does require a great deal of thought for the consequences. Is the company really going to be able to live with a predator-proof scheme if the takeover does not materialise? Perhaps Maud and Roger should have another tête-à-tête before the deed is executed.

First published in *Pensions Management*, May 1987

# CHAPTER 4

# Duties of Trustees

## To get to know the scheme

A new trustee must first of all familiarise himself or herself with the rules of the scheme, the assets and the members. The trustee will need to study the booklet, and read the trust deed and rules. He or she should get a list and valuation of the scheme's investments and details of the members. For this purpose members means not only active members but pensioners and deferred pensioners. Deferred pensioners are members who have left the scheme but not taken a transfer of their accrued rights to a new scheme or a personal pension. They thus have an entitlement to a preserved pension from the scheme when they retire. The new trustee should also study the latest actuarial valuation and the trustees' last annual report. He or she will face an onerous task; one that should not be undertaken lightly.

## Conflicts of interest

The trustee may face conflicts of interest. He or she will probably be an employee of the company and may be one of its directors. He or she could be a member of a trade union or be a union official. The trustee will probably be a member of the scheme. There will then be conflicting loyalties between his or her duties to the union, or to the company, and to the scheme. Trustees have to learn to split themselves in two and separate their roles. When wearing the trustee's hat, the individual must address only the interests of the members. He or she must not act in the interests of the company. The interests of a trade union are not necessarily the same as those of the scheme members and, as such, those interests must be put aside. A trustee's duty is not normally to negotiate benefit improvements for the members but to administer the pension scheme in accordance with the rules. Accordingly he must see that the scheme is operated as provided in the trust deed and rules.

## Main duties

The principal duties of a pension scheme trustee can be summarised as follows:

### To hold the assets of the scheme for the benefit of the members

For example, the trustees should carefully check the credentials of someone claiming a benefit. Is the person claiming to be the member's spouse, and so entitled to a spouse's pension, really the legal spouse. Birth and marriage certificates have to be checked to establish the relationship.

### To act impartially towards all the beneficiaries

This means that not only have the interests of active members (people still in employment) to be considered, but also those of pensioners (those who have retired), and deferred pensioners (who have left the employer with an entitlement to a preserved pension from the scheme and who have not taken a transfer payment). There is a danger that the interests of deferred pensioners in particular will get overlooked. The employer is not interested in them; after all, they have left his or her employment. The trustees cannot take that attitude.

### To carry out their duties with reasonable care and good faith

They must not be careless or act otherwise than in the best interests of all the members.

### To obtain and consider proper expert advice in areas where the trustees themselves are not experts

Typical examples of this duty relate to actuarial matters, investment decisions and questions requiring legal advice. Where the trustees are making a transfer payment, they must obtain the advice of their actuary on its amount. Investment is considered to be a specialised field best left to the expert. Trustees should not therefore make investment decisions without taking advice from an expert. This is dealt with in more detail in Chapter 6. Where legal questions arise, the trustees should consult their lawyer. While trustees are obliged to obtain and consider expert advice, they should not merely rubber stamp it. That would be as bad as not taking the advice in the first place. Experts have as great a capacity to be wrong as anyone else. Clearly there are dangers in ignoring the advice of experts, especially if they prove to be right after all. It is not possible to lay down hard and fast rules, but a degree of discretion has to be exercised.

### To see that money owed to the scheme is paid

The problem here is unpaid contributions, usually from the employer. Employee contributions are deducted from pay by the employer and handed over with the company contributions to the trustees at regular intervals. That, at any rate, is how life should be. It sometimes happens, however, that an employer gets into financial difficulties and, in effect, borrows the employee contributions for the purposes of the business. Ultimately, if all goes well, both employee and company contributions are passed over to the trustees for investment. If all goes badly, this does not happen, the employer becomes insolvent and the contributions are lost. In such a situation the trustees face great difficulties. If they push the employer too hard, they may force him or her into liquidation. This will result in the termination of the scheme and the members will lose their jobs. The trustees will not be thanked for their pains by anyone. On the other hand if they are too relaxed and the employer goes into liquidation, the result will be exactly the same and they may be sued for breach of trust. At the very least, the trustees will have lost the investment return which those unpaid contributions should have been earning. These situations do occur and place the trustees in a nightmarish situation. If the employer becomes insolvent there are certain limited rights of recourse against the Government Redundancy Fund and the trustees will be preferential creditors. But this is not as good as having got the money in and invested.

### To record the transactions and proceedings of the scheme.

This means that the trustees should keep proper accounts of the income and outgoings of the scheme and have them audited by a professionally qualified auditor. The accounts and the auditor's statement must accompany the trustees' annual report. Trustees must also keep minutes of their meetings and record the decisions taken by them.

# CHAPTER 5

# The Trustees' Discretionary Powers

## Why trustees have discretions

If every eventuality were written down in the rules, the rules would be even longer and more complicated than they are now. And so trustees are given discretions to deal with certain matters not covered by the rules or only covered in general terms. Some discretionary powers require a decision in principle: for example, should the scheme accept transfer payments from another scheme. Once that decision has been made, there is no need to consider each case. Other powers require an individual decision in each case: for example, to whom should the trustees pay the discretionary lump sum death benefit payable on death in service. Here the trustees must make proper enquiries before exercising their discretion. Let us examine these discretionary powers in more detail, starting first with decisions in principle.

## Decisions in principle

### Transfer payments

Transfer payments now have to be made on the member's request to other pension schemes approved by the Inland Revenue or to a buy-out policy or a personal pension when a member leaves the scheme with two or more years' qualifying service. Even here, however, although the transfer payment has to be calculated in accordance with the Transfer Value Regulations, the trustees have to take certain decisions. Should their actuary take discretionary pension increases into account when doing the calculation? If the trustees do not tell the actuary to ignore these, they will have to be taken into account. And so the trustees must reach a decision and inform the actuary. It would clearly be a misuse of their powers if they varied the decision from case to case. They must reach a decision in principle which can be applied to all cases. Although trustees must permit transfers out of the scheme, they cannot be compelled to accept transfer payments in. Usually they do so and they should make a policy decision about this. They should also settle in principle what benefits they will give in return — added years of pensionable service or an additional amount of pension. This is an area where actuarial advice will be needed. Having made their decision, the pension manager or the actuary should be able to apply it in each individual case without having to refer back to the trustees. It should be borne in mind that the method of calculation of transfers out has to be consistent with transfers in.

## Late entry

Should the trustees permit someone who has left the scheme, or who has not joined it when he or she was first eligible to do so, to join or rejoin later. Sometimes the rules regulate this and permit one or two second chances. But often the matter is left to the trustees' discretion. This is an area where they should probably reach a policy decision. If only future service rights are to be granted, they may well feel that, as long as a satisfactory medical report has been obtained, they should permit late entry. If the employer wants the trustees to grant back service, then an individual decision will have to be made. This aspect is considered under the heading "Augmentation". Medical evidence is needed, if only to satisfy the scheme's insurers, before the late entrant can be covered for death in service benefits. Accordingly, late entry may require both a decision in principle, with an individual decision in a particular case if there are questions about the medical evidence or of granting past service rights.

## Commutation

Sometimes scheme rules give the member the right to take a tax-free lump sum on retirement. Part of the pension will have to be given up to provide for the lump sum. Often the rules give the trustees a discretion both to permit this and to fix the amount of the lump sum. If this is the case, the trustees should not make individual decisions. They should settle the commutation factors in conjunction with their actuary and decide that commutation on that basis will be open to all members. It would clearly be inequitable to allow commutation in some cases, but not in others.

## Early retirement

Scheme rules sometimes give the member the right to retire on or after age 50 or even earlier on grounds of ill-health. Sometimes this option requires the consent of the employer or of the trustees. This again is an area where individual decisions would be seen as being unfair. If the early retirement pension is reduced to take account of early payment, a cost factor will not be involved. There are, of course, employment considerations, which is why the employer may want to be consulted and to give consent. That aside, there is no reason why the trustees should not reach a policy decision about such cases. If ill-health retirement or redundancy arises, an actuarial reduction to the pension need not be applied. If so, that will impose a cost burden on the scheme. If this has not been taken into account by the actuary in recommending the rate of contributions, the trustees should not permit early retirement unless they are satisfied that money is available to meet the cost.

## Pension increases

Often the trustees are given power at their discretion to increase pensions in payment. It would normally be a breach of trust to give some members, but not others, a pension increase. That is not to say that trustees cannot distinguish between different classes of members. For example, members who retired in the 1970s might be given an additional increase to compensate for the hyper inflation of that decade. The trustees should not, however, make individual decisions in this area. The rules will often require the trustees to obtain the employer's consent before giving an increase. This is because there is a cost factor involved. The extra money has to be found from extra contributions or out of any surplus in the scheme. Whether or not the rules require the employer's consent, the trustees should, because of the financial implications, consult the employer and also the actuary.

## Individual decisions

Individual decisions are required in the following areas:

## Death benefits

Lump sum benefits — usually a multiple of the member's pay — are nearly always held on discretionary trusts for the member's relatives or dependants. They are not usually payable as of right to the member's spouse or to a nominated beneficiary. This method of payment is used to avoid inheritance tax. The member is given the right to nominate his or her chosen beneficiary to receive the lump sum benefit. But this does not bind the trustees, although they should give it serious weight when deciding how to exercise their discretion. The Inland Revenue requires the trustees to make their decision within two years of the member's death, failing which the money has to be paid to the member's estate. This is an area where knowledge of the member's family and financial circumstances is essential before a sensible decision can be reached. In most cases the member's nomination form will be followed. But what if there isn't one or it is out of date? What if the member's nomination is unreasonable, for example, if he or she nominates the cats' home and is survived by a wife and children. There are no hard and fast rules. Trustees must act honestly and reasonably and set aside their own political, religious or moral views or prejudices. They must not discriminate on these grounds. But so long as they reach their decision fairly, having made proper enquiries, on the basis of knowledge of the member's family and other circumstances, their decision will not be disturbed by the courts. It is sensible not to give or record reasons for their decisions, although the decision itself must be recorded in the trustees' minutes. For some illustrations of the problems that can arise, readers are referred to "Judgement and Justice" which follows this chapter.

## Augmentation

Trustees are often given power to increase or augment the benefits payable to a member or beneficiary. Sometimes the employer's consent is required because of the financial implications. Increasing benefits costs money. Someone has to pay. And so, as with pension increases, whether or not the rules require the trustees to obtain the employer's consent, they would be wise to consult both the employer and the actuary. In any event, it is usually the company that triggers a request for augmentation. They may want, for example, to provide for the retirement on full pension of certain senior executives at age 60 or 62, when the normal retirement date is 65. If there is sufficient money in the scheme, or if the employer agrees to pay the additional contributions recommended by the actuary, should the trustees agree to the employer's request? This is an area which frequently causes great problems to trustees. The favoured members are usually senior, better paid, employees. Why should they be given better benefits than the rest of the members? The answer is that so long as there is no disadvantage to the other members, there is no reason why not, and indeed every reason why, the trustees should agree. It must be remembered that the employer did not have to establish the pension scheme in the first place, that he or she can usually reduce, suspend or terminate contributions and that the employer may, depending on the rules, be able to trigger a winding-up of the scheme. It is therefore in the interests of the members as a whole not to lose the employer's goodwill. Trustees should normally, therefore, exercise their powers of augmentation on the employer's request, so long as the other members are not disadvantaged.

## Rule changes

Most pension schemes give the employer and the trustees jointly power to change the rules. This power must be exercised by the trustees in the interests of all the beneficiaries — current members, early leavers and pensioners. No one class should be left out of consideration. The trustees must be even handed. This does not mean that all members must share equally in benefit improvements, merely that the trustees must give consideration to the different classes of members and ensure that their interests are taken into account. For example, if it is decided that a given amount of money should be allocated to benefit improvements, the trustees should ask the actuary to cost out a number of different options. They may wish to guarantee a certain level of pension increases, or to increase the rate at which they grant discretionary increases. They may wish to improve the death in service benefits or improve the rate at which pensions accrue. They may well take a different view about deferred pensioners — those who have left the employer's service. They may feel that some greater measure of revaluation should be applied than the statutory minimum, or they may feel, having regard to their length of service, that that is enough. Their interests must be thought about but that does not mean that the trustees must give them benefit improvements, or benefit improvements of equivalent value. But they must not be overlooked.

This is another area where no hard and fast lines can be laid down. It is a matter for the trustees' discretion and as long as they act fairly, their decision will not be overturned. Often the impetus for benefit improvements comes from the employer. As long as the trustees are satisfied, having taken actuarial advice, that the money needed to pay for the improvements is either available or will be forthcoming, they should usually agree. If in doubt, the trustees should obtain advice from their experts.

Readers are referred to "The Lawyer's Tale: Winding Down", which follows this chapter, for an illustration of some of the problems that can arise in the exercise of trustees' discretionary powers.

# The Lawyer's Tale:
# Judgement and Justice

John Watson was one of the senior pension superintendents at the Magnificent Mutual Life Assurance Society. He was young, enthusiastic and fussed around his team like a mother hen. Back at work fresh from the Christmas and New Year break, he was ready to tackle the new world of personal pensions, free standing AVCs, contracted-out money purchase schemes and all the rest of the 1988 pensions revolution.

But none of these was really his immediate problem. He had just taken a telephone call from Colonel Braithwaite, the managing director of United Widgets, one of the most prestigious of Magnificent Mutual's pension schemes. The scheme had recently run into a number of difficulties over discretionary death benefits, and it was suggested that a visit from John might help sort out the problems.

John decided to take with him Archie Smithers, the Society's lawyer. The two were old friends and had helped each other through many a crisis.

They presented themselves at United Widget's office the following week and met the trustees. These consisted of Colonel Braithwaite, a bluff north countryman who had built up the company's business, Bill Withers, the personnel manager, and the company's accountant Ron Smith. Colonel Braithwaite opened the meeting briskly by saying:

"We've had a lot of deaths recently — mainly old soldiers who were too long in the tooth to be worth their oats. Luckily, since death in service benefits are insured, the Magnificent Mutual foots that bill and the company, quite frankly, will be better off with younger men. The odd thing is that they have made some curious wills and it is giving us no end of bother."

"Not wills," interrupted Ron Smith, "just nomination forms. They are not the same thing at all."

"Pipe down, young man," stormed the Colonel, "You are here as the company's accountant. Don't speak unless you're spoken to."

"What exactly are the problems," intervened John quickly.

"Well," said the Colonel, "Grimes went and left all his benefits to some boyfriend — never mind that he had a wife and three children and Miss Fanshawe in accounts left all hers to a cats' home. To cap it all, one of our foremen, Huxtable, turned out not to be married after all, but we have got some woman from Paisley saying she is his common law wife. If I'd known we would have had all this trouble, I would never have started a pension scheme."

Smithers decided that it was time he stuck his oar in.

"Under the pension scheme rules," he said, "the trustees have complete discretion over paying out these benefits. They can pay them to the member's relatives or dependants in whatever way they choose. Your rules have recently been altered to make various benefit improvements and we took the opportunity to widen the trustees' discretion. As permitted by the Inland Revenue for some years now, these benefits can be paid to clubs, or charities and similar organisations. If there is no one suitable, they can even keep the money in the fund. The member is asked to complete a nomination form giving an expression of his wishes. But this is not binding on the trustees. They must take it into account and they must act reasonably and honestly. As long as they do this, their decision cannot be set aside. Do you not agree, Mr Smith?"

Ron blinked nervously, "I am sure what you say is right, Mr Smithers. But I am only an accountant — I don't really know about these things".

"You'd better get your skates on, then, and learn about them," boomed the Colonel, "you can't scratch away at ledgers all day. You should widen your horizons and learn about the real world — not just debits and credits. But I digress. I take it from what you have said, Smithers, that we can do what we like. In that case I vote we send Grimes' boyfriend packing: the money can be left in the scheme. I like that — the Magnificent Mutual pay us out and we keep the money. We mustn't encourage immorality."

"But," said Smithers quickly, "it isn't as simple as that. First, Grimes left a wife and three children. Secondly, he left a nomination form in favour of his friend. I am not suggesting that you should follow it slavishly, but you should take it into account. You cannot possibly keep the money in the fund. That is only permitted by the rules if the member left no relatives or dependants — which is not the case here. If you don't pay the money to the friend, you should surely pay it to his wife and children. It is your decision of course — not mine", he added quickly, sensing the Colonel's temper.

"Quite," said the Colonel. "Well, we'll pay it to Mrs Grimes. Now what about old Miss Fanshawe? You are not going to tell me we have got to pay four times her salary of £10,000 to a lot of cats?"

"From one old cat to another" quipped Bill Withers. The Colonel chose to ignore that remark.

"No," said Smithers, "but is there anyone else? Did she leave any parents, brothers or sisters, nephews or nieces? Were any of them dependent on her? You've really got to know all that before you can make a decision."

"She did live with an elderly sister, who has a small pension but nothing else. I think that but for Miss Fanshawe, she would have been in an old people's home."

"Well, why did she nominate the cats' home?", asked Smithers. "It seems a little perverse."

"It is not perverse," shouted the Colonel, "it is perverted — I am not going to let our money, or even the Magnificent Mutual's, be paid to a bunch of mangy cats."

Bill Withers interrupted to explain that Miss Fanshawe's nomination had been made many years ago and that she had told him she had meant to change it many times. He suggested therefore that, in these circumstances, they might ignore the nomination and give the money to the sister. They all quickly agreed with this suggestion.

"That leaves our foreman," said Bill. "His situation is a little more complicated. Before he joined us, he formed a liaison with a woman in Paisley where they lived together as man and wife for many years. Indeed, everyone thought they were married and their neighbours in Paisley had looked on them in this light. He lost his job in Paisley, came south to us but neglected to bring this woman and their two children. He then formed a similar liaison with a woman in England and lived with her until he died. He had a further two children by her.

"Neither Mrs Huxtable produced a marriage certificate. The first one did produce an opinion from a Scottish lawyer — a Writer to the Signet no less — who opined, no doubt for a handsome fee, that she was the lawful widow having established a valid marriage under Scottish law by 'cohabitation and repute'. What is more the DSS agreed and were paying her a widow's pension. Perhaps wisely the foreman had neglected to complete any nomination form."

"Right," said the Colonel, "if Huxtable couldn't make up his mind, why should we? Presumably, if the Scottish lawyer johnny was right, *numero uno* will get a widow's pension and her children will get orphans' pensions under the rules. Number two was not nominated by him and can be safely ignored. The fund will keep the lump sum death benefit."

"But," Bill cut in quickly, "the second Mrs Huxtable lived with him for 20 years and bore him two children. She always appeared at the Christmas dinner dance. She clearly can't get a widow's pension and her children aren't eligible for orphans' pensions. Surely you wouldn't send her away with a flea in her ear? Could we not give her the lump sum benefit?"

"Oh, all right," said the Colonel testily. "We have gone on long enough with this discussion. Now, Smithers, you had better give us some guidelines for the future so that we know what to do in these cases."

"Right," said Smithers "let me make a few simple points:
— first, check if there is a nomination and when it was made;
— if there is no nomination, the trustees have a completely free hand. They should investigate the family background and circumstances and then decide fairly and reasonably who should have the money;
— if there is a nomination, they should normally follow it, unless it is out of date or thoroughly perverse — in which case they should act in accordance with their own judgment;
— trustees should remember that bodies such as clubs and charities can benefit and these should be borne in mind especially in the case of unmarried members;
— trustees should not allow their prejudices — political, sexual or religious — to cloud their judgment;
— they should not seek to retain the money in the fund and make a windfall profit. Retaining the money should only be done to defeat the claims of the Crown to *bona vacantia* — unclaimed monies. It is simply a long stop device;
— trustees should not usually give their reasons. If they do, they might be used as a launching pad for upsetting their decision — better to remain silent;
— finally, they should make their decision within the two year time limit allowed by the Inland Revenue."

First published in *Pensions Management*, February 1988.

# The Lawyer's Tale: Winding Down

Douglas Livingstone was one of the new breed of pension superintendents at the Magnificent Mutual. He had been promoted after the early
retirement of the old General Manager, Monty Murgatroyd. Young,
with a thick shock of long hair, glasses, a conservative chalk stripe
grey suit, he looked every inch a pensions administrator. One of his
pension schemes was the Great American Dream UK Pension Plan.
Unfortunately the Great American Dream had not worked out, at any
rate in the United Kingdom. The company had ceased trading, closed
the last of its ice cream parlours and Doug was given the job of
winding up the pension scheme. Although the company was solvent,
there were no employees left. The pension scheme had about 100
current and deferred pensioners.

Wind ups had caused a lot of bother recently for the Magnificent
Mutual; and so Doug decided to consult Archie Smithers at Docs
Galore about the problems. Docs Galore was the specialist pension law
boutique which the Magnificent Mutual used to sub-contract its
documentation work.

When Doug arrived for the meeting, Archie introduced him to their
latest recruit, a tall but solidly built young man called Simon, and said
that he would be helping on this particular scheme.

"Don't you ever do any work any more?" asked Doug sarcastically.
They were old sparring partners but under the surface banter each had
a healthy respect for the other.

"Well, yes, quite a lot. But I've read the file and since the surplus
here is only £75,000, it will soon evaporate if I spend too much time on
the case," replied Archie with a breezy laugh.

"Well, what about my old mate, Dave? Does he do any work or is he
off swanning on another of his overseas sports tours? I must admit I've
never known such a pair as you two for not sitting behind your
desks!" said Doug.

"Come, come," replied Archie a trifle testily. "Even if we're not in the office five days a week, it doesn't mean we're not working. David has got the job of winding up the 22 schemes of the old Carpet Bonanza Company that went bust last year. He's secretary to the independent trustees and that's virtually a full time job. As it happens he's in today and I've asked him to join us for lunch afterwards."

"Well, that's different then," said Doug. "I didn't know you'd booked a table for lunch. I'd best get on. It's all quite simple really. Once we've bought out the benefits of all the pensions and deferreds, there's a surplus of £75,000. There are some sticky fingers back in Providence, Rhode Island, where the US parent company is, who want that repatriated smartish."

"But," said Simon, "if I may be so bold as to interrupt, you've got to give LPI pension increases before you can refund any money to the company. You will no doubt recall," he continued, winding himself up, "that Section 11 of the Social Security Act 1990 restricts payments to employers out of pension scheme resources until LPI on all pensions has been granted. And this applies to schemes which are winding up as well as continuing schemes."

"Where do you get them from, Archie?" asked Doug with heavy irony. "Don't teach your grandmother to suck eggs. I did know that. And it's been done, and there's still £75,000 left. May I continue?"

Poor Simon went bright red.

"Well," continued Doug, "the trustees and the company feel that as all the members have got their benefits bought out in full, plus LPI, that's enough and the rest should go back to the company. The winding up rule gives the trustees discretion to augment benefits up to Revenue limits. Any surplus after that goes back, of course to, the company."

"Do the trustees have an unfettered discretion?" asked Simon rather rashly.

"If I could be left to finish the story, we might all get to lunch a bit quicker," said Doug. "No, they don't. That's the point. They've got to get the company's consent. What's more, the old rules when the scheme was first set up in 1970 only required the trustees to act 'in consultation with the company'. That got changed to company consent when you did your consolidated trust deed and rules back in 1986, Archie. I don't know why you changed it, but you did."

"That's easy," replied Archie. "I changed the standard because Philip, the pensions actuary, and I both thought the standard was too member-biased; so we redressed the balance in a number of areas to give more powers to the company."

"And you didn't tell anyone about all this, did you?" said Doug.

Yes, we told all the pension superintendents at the next monthly meeting," replied Archie indignantly.

"That's not the point, you old cloth head; you didn't bother to tell the company or the trustees when you dished out your new standard, did you?" said Doug.

"Look here," replied Archie, "not so much of your lip, young man. I don't work for the Magnificent Mutual any more, you know. I don't have to put up with that sort of thing."

"Yes, you do," said Doug with a grin. "I pay you - not the other way round. Shall I get back to the story. Some of the members have gone off to see a solicitor. Unfortunately he's a member of the Association of Pension Lawyers and he seems to know what he's talking about. He's advised the members that the rule change in 1986 was invalid, because the trustees weren't told about it and would have objected if they'd been told. So the trustees need only consult with the company. That's not much of an obstacle because the trustees can still go away and do what they wanted to in the first place."

"Who are the trustees?" asked Simon

"I wondered when you'd get round to that," said Doug. "Well, there are three. The first is Hank Western from the parent company in Providence. He's a cigar toting Texan and has clearly defined ideas about the ownership of surplus. He also regards LPI as symptomatic of terminal communism. Then there's the company secretary, Bernard Jones, a fussy little man with a nervous tic and a bow tie. He'd never say boo to a goose, let alone Hank. And last, but not least, there's old Rainey, the company's whingeing bank manager. Since the company's got a large overdraft, the last thing he wants is to see the surplus go to the members. And so, they won't change their minds and give any more to the members. The members' solicitor is about to issue a writ against the trustes and has asked the Magnificent Mutual to undertake not to part with the scheme's assets. We're in a real pickle."

"What exactly is the lawyer saying?" asked Archie.

"Well, there's pages of it. Here's the file," replied Doug. "But basically he says that:

(a) the trustees never had a proper meeting to discuss augmenta-
    tion. Hank just told them what to do on the phone;

(b) the trustees looked at the new winding up rule, requiring the

company's consent, when they should have looked at the old
one which only required consultation;

(c) the trustees' primary duty is to the members. They must
augment benefits up to Revenue limits before giving anything
to the company."

"Rubbish," said Simon. "There'd be no point in giving trustees a
discretion to augment benefits if that were right. In any event it's
quite clear from the Icarus case that trustees can give the surplus back
to the company. The trustees have got to act responsibly. This means
that they must:

— decide whether or not to exercise their powers;
— find out all the relevant facts; and
— then decide in good faith whether or not to augment."

"Well said," muttered Archie approvingly. "What about the rule
change, though?"

"On this point I agree with the members' solicitor," said Simon.
"The Mettoy case decided that in circumstances like this the rule
change was invalid. But I'm not sure that since the latest Imperial
Tobacco case there's all that much difference between 'consent' and
'consultation'. The judge in that case decided that the company could
give or withold its consent to pension increases, acting purely in its
own interests. In other words it was a 'beneficial' power, not a
'fiduciary' one. A fiduciary power is a power that has to be exercised
in the interests of the members — in a trustee like fashion. Whereas a
beneficial power is one that the company can exercise in the interests
of the proprietors — the shareholders."

"I don't know what you're on about," said Doug with a touch of
irritation. "If it was a beneficial power, the company could ignore the
members."

"Not so," said Simon. "The judge, Sir Nicolas Browne-Wilkinson,
the senior judge of the chancery division of the High Court, said the
company must conduct itself in such a way as not to destroy the
relationship of trust and confidence between employer and employee
without reasonable and proper cause."

"Archie, can you explain all this mumbo jumbo?" asked Doug.

"Well, I'll try," replied Archie. "That's why I don't think the rule
change made that much difference. The company can't just consider
its own selfish interests. It must consider the members as well."

"For goodness' sake, you two. What does all this mean? Have the trustees got to do more for the members or not?" cried Doug with ill-concealed fury.

"Let's just consider the first point before we go back to your question," said Archie. "Yet another case decided recently — the Fisons Pension Scheme case — showed that to reach a proper decision trustees must:

— consider all the relevant data;
— look at the appropriate rule of the pension scheme;
— take proper legal and actuarial advice; and
— lastly take decisions at a properly constituted meeting.

"If the decision can be impeached on any of these grounds, it will be set aside. It looks to me as if the trustees fell foul of just about all these rules here."

Doug cut in: "Sounds like another lawyer's bonanza to me. For heaven's sake stop quoting cases and tell me what to do."

"Well," said Archie, "if I were you, I'd tell the trustees to start again, hold a proper meeting; consider, for example, what it would cost to provide Revenue maximum benefits; consider the views of the company and then reach a decision. To be on the safe side, they should rely on the old rule and 'consult'. Although as Simon said, I'm not sure it makes much difference after the Imps case. To be blunt, if the trustees don't do better next time, they'll end up in court and the lawyers will spend the surplus."

"No wonder you and Dave ride round in Jags and Porsches," said Doug. "You can pay for lunch."

On that happy note David appeared and they went to the Ritz.

"I agree," said David pacifically to his old friend Doug, "that everything used to be much simpler and we were all happy. But complications do have some advantages. Life is certainly more interesting and much more profitable. Let's drink to the lessons from the cases!"

First published in *Pensions Management*, January 1991.

# CHAPTER 6

# Investment Powers

## The investment rules

Trustees must act in accordance with the terms of the investment rules of their scheme; they must also act with due prudence. The first test is whether the proposed investment is authorised. Nowadays pension scheme trust deeds and rules confer wide powers of investment on trustees. It is still necessary to check, however, that they are authorised to enter into, for example, subunderwriting contracts or traded options. If the trust rules are up to date, they probably will be. It could be that an old fashioned scheme limits the amount which can be invested in equities. Such schemes do exist. It is a point to be watched and may need to be checked by an expert. If a scheme does not have a wide investment power, then the position is regulated by the Trustee Investments Act 1961 which says that half the scheme's assets must be invested in gilt edged securities; the other half can be invested in equities.

## The prudent man

If the trustees can, under the rules, make the proposed investment, should they? The law says that the trustees must look after trustee investments as if they were looking after them for someone else. One may take risks on one's own behalf, but must be more careful with other people's money. The trustees have to act with due prudence.

## The best interests of the beneficiaries

Trustees must put aside their own personal interests and views. They must put the best interests of their beneficiaries first, and normally the best interests of the beneficiaries are their financial interests. These points are illustrated by the case of *Cowan v Scargill* in 1984 — the National Union of Mineworkers case. The mineworkers' pension scheme had a five year investment plan which was up for review. The investment managers were suggesting that more money should be invested overseas and in oil and gas stocks. The scheme had five union trustees and five management trustees and no provisions for breaking a deadlock. The union trustees opposed the investment manager's proposals because they thought the money should be invested in this country, not overseas, and in the coal industry, not in competing industries. The judge did not uphold their views. The mineworkers' scheme had a good proportion of members who had retired and were pensioners, plus many members who had left the industry but kept an entitlement to a preserved pension in the scheme — pensioners and deferred pensioners. It was not in their best financial interests to invest money in the coal industry if a better return could be obtained elsewhere. And so the judge decided in favour of the management trustees, who agreed with the investment manager's report.

# Expert advice

Trustees must obtain and take heed of proper expert investment advice. The obligation is to take heed of it, not necessarily to follow it. Trustees must be wary of rubber stamping the advice of their experts.

# Diversifying investments

Trustees must have regard to the need for diversification of investments. They should not put all their eggs in one basket. If they do this and are successful, they will be acclaimed. If they fail, they will face the risk of being sued for breach of trust.

# Investments must be suitable

Trustees must hold investments which are in themselves suitable. For example, an investment in a brothel or a casino would not strike one at first sight as an entirely suitable investment for trustees whose duties include looking after widows and orphans. Not only must the investments be suitable in themselves, they must also be suitable having regard to the scheme's liabilities. An example of this would be an investment in property when a number of members are coming up to retirement age. A trustee has occasionally to look, as it were, over his or her shoulders, to see what is coming up on the horizon. If in a small scheme a number of members are due to retire shortly, there will be a need for cash to pay the tax-free lump sums and, perhaps, purchase annuities for them. Putting all the scheme's spare cash in an office block would hardly facilitate this. Property is notoriously difficult to realise quickly. Putting the money on deposit would be more suitable having regard to the scheme's liabilities.

# Self-investment

A worry for trustees arises when the employer suggests self-investment. Self-investment occurs when the trustees buy shares in the employer or lend money to the employer or buy property for occupation by the employer. Any such transaction must be carried out at arm's length, with the benefit of independent professional advice and on ordinary commercial terms. Nevertheless, self-investment places trustees in a conflict of interest, where their duties and loyalties can be divided. The National Association of Pension Funds has therefore recommended complete avoidance of self-investment by pension scheme trustees. Trustees should check the investment rule, if self-investment is proposed, to see if there are any restrictions on their powers. There could well be.

The Social Security Act 1990 for the first time gives power to regulate self-investment or investment in "employer-related assets". The Act gives the Secretary of State for Social Services power to limit investments in employer-related assets. These include:
(a) shares and securities in the employer;
(b) land or property used by the employer;
(c) loans to the employer (including unpaid scheme contributions).
Regulations have now been issued which limit employer-related investments to 5% of the assets of the scheme. Any existing loans and quoted securities within this category will have to be reduced to the 5% limit within two years. For shares quoted on the unlisted Securities Market the period for compliance is five years. There is no

time limit for reducing other forms of employer–related investment, for example property.

The regulations do not apply to schemes which —

(a) have less than 12 members who are all trustees of the scheme; and

(b) have a rule that any decision to invest in employer-related investments has to be agreed in writing by all the members.

"The Lawyer's Tale: Solution for a Surplus", which follows this chapter, was first published in June 1988 before the regulations were made. The trustees will now have to get the company to reduce the loan to 5% within two years.

# The Lawyer's Tale: Solution for a Surplus

Following the death of its pensions actuary, the Magnificent Mutual had been looking for a replacement. Good actuaries are hard to come by and Montague Murgatroyd, the Magnificent Mutual's chief general manager, was getting desperate. There was no one in house who was suitable. Archie Smithers, the Society's lawyer, seeing the salary being offered, was heard muttering enviously that a monkey with a calculator could do the job. Eventually, however, old Murgatroyd recruited a young man called Colin Bell.

Colin was a Yorkshireman who wore check suits that Murgatroyd thought more suitable for a bookie than an actuary. But then, he reflected, perhaps there was not so much difference between the two professions. They both make assessments of future probabilities, although actuaries don't have to carry the can for their mistakes!

Colin had a broad accent, an infectious laugh and was an immediate hit both with his colleagues and clients.

One day, Colonel Braithwaite of United Widgets rang to say he was having a spot of bother with the bank. The company had a temporary cash flow problem and it was up against its overdraft limit. The manager would not play ball. So the Colonel turned to his old friend John Watson, the Magnificent Mutual pensions superintendent, who looked after the United Widgets pension scheme.

John was the sort of person you instinctively turn to in times of trouble. The Colonel reminded John that the pension scheme's latest actuarial valuation had thrown up a surplus of £1m; all he needed was a loan of £500,000 to tide him through.

"Rainey, the bank manager, is one of those whingers who won't lend you money when you need it, but when you don't he is always trying to sell you a soft loan", said the Colonel, "A typical fair weather friend".

John knew the Colonel too well to try and elicit all the facts in the course of a telephone call. So he suggested that he should go and see the Colonel and take the opportunity of introducing Colin, the new actuary.

The following day, John and Colin presented themselves at the Colonel's office at 10 o'clock. The Colonel had his accountant there and he quickly presented the facts. The company had an overdraft limit of £1m and was right up to the limit. It needed a further £500,000 fairly speedily. The bank's loan was fully secured by a mortgage on the company's freehold factory site, which was conservatively valued at £2m. The accountant patiently explained that the company's financial position was basically sound, the order book was full and business was profitable. It had recently secured a couple of big export orders and although it needed money for materials and wages now, it would not get paid until the orders were fulfilled in six months' time.

The accountant had hit on the bright idea of repaying the pension scheme's surplus £1 m to the company. True, there would be a tax charge of £400,000, but the company would be left with £600,000 free money to tide it over the temporary difficulty. John and Colin both knew that it wasn't the time to start explaining to the Colonel that the Revenue required a 5% margin of solvency in the case of an employer's refund. Apart from upsetting the Colonel, it would not really have affected the figures because £950,000 was for all practical purposes as good as £1 m.

John and Colin thought this over quickly. If you took more than ten seconds over a question, the Colonel's highly polished shoes began to twitch with impatience.

"Well", said Colin, "that sounds all right to me. The pension scheme is in good shape and a refund of that magnitude would be permitted by the Revenue. There could be legal problems, however. We need to know whether your scheme rules prohibit a refund to the company and whether we could alter the rules to allow this. May I give Archie Smithers a ring to check on the position?"

Archie said he would check on the United Widget's trust deed and rules and ring them back. Being an efficient man, he was back to them within five minutes.

"I am afraid", said Smithers, "that your rules not only prevent a refund being made to the company but they also stop any rule change to permit this".

Colin interrupted on the conference phone to say: "But I thought that the Social Security Act 1986 gave the Secretary of State power to issue regulations to enable the Occupational Pensions Board to make modification orders overriding scheme rules? What's more, I seem to remember seeing draft regulations on this very subject a few months ago. You do remember that, don't you Archie?"

Smithers smiled and continued: "Yes, indeed I do. It's all right. I am not yet suffering from senile dementia". Why is it, thought Smithers, that actuaries always think they know better than everyone else.

"The regulations", Smithers went on, "have not been issued because it has been pointed out to the DSS that the primary legislation — the 1986 Act, which in turn amended the Social Security Act 1973 — said that such a modification order could not be made if it would result in any existing or prospective entitlement of a member being diminished without his consent. If an overfunded scheme were to be wound up, the members could benefit from the surplus being used to augment their benefits. Therefore a modification order could not be made to allow a refund of surplus to the employer, because this would defeat the members' rights on winding up. And so the regulations have never been made. It is up to the Government to amend the primary legislation in due course".

Archie was sufficiently astute to know that the messenger of bad news invariably got shot. He also knew that the Colonel wanted solutions — not explanations — and so he invited himself to lunch with the Colonel, John and Colin. "If I can't come up with an answer, I'll buy the lunch", ended Smithers. And so an hour later he appeared, scarcely restraining the smile on his face.

He addressed the assembled company: "Why don't you get the pension scheme to lend you the money. There is a surplus of £1 million. You only need half that. There is ample security for the loan. You'd just as soon pay interest at 2% over base rate to the pension fund as to the bank. The company could repay the loan over a five year period."

"That sounds excellent, Archie," said John "but what about the trustees? Can they allow this and even if they can, should they?"

Archie smiled tolerantly: "Your basic instinct is absolutely sound John, but I have checked the trust deed and rules and the trustees have a wide power of investment. This includes loans to the company so long as a commercial rate of interest is paid. But I agree that the trustees have got to decide whether or not they should exercise this power. They must not put all their eggs in one basket.

"However, the money in question only represents 15% of the scheme's assets and the company is basically sound. There is good security for the loan, which would only be for five years at the most, a good rate of interest would be paid and the investment would be good for the company and its employees and, to that extent, the members.

"Since the company can take a contribution holiday for five years, it can repay the loan by monthly instalments equal to the amount of the company's contributions it was not having to pay. As these amount to £100,000 a year, foregoing the contribution holiday would repay the loan. The only risk is if the company goes down the tube before the loan is repaid. But against this, it is a reducing loan and there is ample security. On balance, therefore, I think that the loan would be a proper and prudent exercise of the trustees' investment powers".

"My goodness, you do go on", said the Colonel. "But this time I find what you say more interesting than usual!"

"But what about the Revenue and the OPB?", said Colin.

"You don't have to worry about them", said Archie. "As the scheme is not a small self-administered scheme, there is no need to notify the Revenue. So far as the OPB is concerned, I agree that the loan would be regarded both as self-investment and a concentration of investments and would have to be notified at the end of the scheme year. But having regard to the figures, the loan would not affect the solvency of the scheme or prejudice the priority liabilities, like guaranteed minimum pensions, if the scheme was wound up. It would not stop you, Colin, from completing your certificate or necessitate your qualifying it. I don't foresee any problems with the OPB".

"Well", said the Colonel, "I think that warrants cracking a few bottles of champagne. Wait till I see old Rainey's face at the bank".

"At the risk of over egging the pudding, may I ask your indulgence for two minutes, Colonel, if only to complete the education of my collea-gues", said Smithers somewhat rashly. The Colonel grunted and said he would make a couple of phone calls while Smithers finished his lecture!

"The concern of the OPB", said Archie, "is to ensure that each contracted-out scheme is funded without undue reliance on self invest-ment and in particular, that in the event of winding up, its resources would be enough to cover GMPs and other priority liabilities. Since the investment would exceed 10% of the scheme's assets, the actuary would have to be given details. But as long as you are satisfied, Colin, that priority liabilities would be fully covered without relying on the self investment, you won't have to qualify your certificate".

"You obviously know the contents of Memorandum 76 by heart", laughed Colin, "and what's more, the company is getting its money immediately and avoiding the 40% tax charge. This is the first time I've ever come across a solution from a pensions lawyer that actually makes life easier. Don't let anyone find out or you'll get struck off!"


First published in *Pensions Management*, June 1988.


Since this article was first published in June 1988 the law has been changed — see Schedule 6 of the Social Security Act 1989, and regulations have been issued — see The Occupational Pension Schemes (Modification) Regulations 1990 and the Occupational Pension Schemes (Investment of Scheme's Resources) Regulations 1991.

# CHAPTER 7

# The Financial Services Act 1986

The Financial Services Act affects pension scheme trustees in the following ways.

## Investment management

### The need for authorisation

The Act regulates investment management and requires investment managers to be authorised or exempt from authorisation. Trustees of pension schemes are regarded as being in the business of managing investments and thus will require to be authorised unless they delegate all investment management or all day to day investment management to someone who is authorised or exempt. Most trustees will not want to become authorised. It requires an application to the Investment Management Regulatory Organisation (IMRO) for which fees have to be paid each year. Few trustees have felt this to be necessary. In practice most trustees do delegate all investment management or day to day investment management to someone who is authorised, such as a merchant bank or an insurance company.

### Day to day investment management

Not many trustees will want to delegate *all* investment management. What then does delegating "day to day" investment management mean? There is no definition in the 1986 Act but the Securities and Investments Board — the body responsible for implementing the Act —

has given guidance. Day to day decisions do not include strategic decisions such as portfolio weighting; for example, how much money is invested overseas (in other words the big decisions).

### Decisions the trustees can take

Trustees can also require to be consulted in certain circumstances, for example:
  (a)   in a takeover;
  (b)   where the investment manager has a conflict of interest;
  (c)   concerning certain sensitive decisions like buying shares in a competitor;
  (d)   when policy considerations are involved — for example, should the trustees buy shares in tobacco companies or in South African concerns?

### Frequent interventions by trustees

It is a question of degree so that frequent interventions by the trustees outside the regular investment review meetings would probably amount to day to day investment management. The initial decision by the trustees to invest in, say, a managed fund policy would be regarded as strategic. If the trustees want to exercise their rights to switch between funds, it all depends on how often the trustees want to do this and how much detail they get involved in. If they switch no more than three or four times a year, that is regarded as being a strategic decision. Decisions on how much of the fund goes into equities, property, etc are also regarded as strategic; but if the trustees get involved in picking particular funds or unit trusts, the decisions could, especially if they are taken frequently, be regarded as day to day investment management and so require authorisation.

# Advice on investments

Trustees are often asked to advise a member about joining or leaving the scheme, about the various options open to an early leaver and about paying additional contributions. If the trustees are engaged in the business of advising on investments, they will need to be authorised by one of the recognised regulatory bodies. There are two aspects:

### The business of investment advice

If the trustees are paid, for example by receiving commission, then they will be regarded as being in the business of giving investment advice. If they do not get paid but give advice frequently and systematically, they will still be regarded as being in business. But if they do not get paid and only give advice on an irregular and unsystematic basis, they will not need to be authorised.

### What is an investment?

Investments exclude property and deposit accounts with a bank or building society and a member's interests under an occupational pension scheme. Rights under a personal pension scheme, unless it is deposit based, will count as investments. It follows from this that trustees can, without fear of transgressing the Act, advise a member on the merits of the occupational scheme as contrasted with personal pensions. But they must not go from general to specific advice about personal pensions. In other words they must not get dragged into advising about particular personal pension products. Trustees can inform early leavers about the options open to them — a preserved pension, a transfer to a new scheme or to a personal pension. But they must not recommend particular buy out policies or personal pensions. They can talk about the differences between the in-house voluntary contribution arrangements (rights under an occupational scheme) and free standing additional voluntary contribution schemes (FSAVCs), which will usually be investments. But, again, they must not advise on the merits of particular FSAVCs.

# Arranging deals in investments

If the trustees are in the business of arranging deals in investments, they will need authorisation. The question of what is meant by being "in business" has already been covered under "Advice on Investments". Trustees will be regarded as arranging deals in investments if, for example, they make arrangements with an insurance company offering a special deal on buy out policies and get paid in commission or fees for doing this. If they do not get paid, they will not normally be regarded as being in business unless they make such arrangements regularly and systematically. Trustees who want to help their members in this way would be safer if they made a special arrangement, not direct, with the provider but with an independent intermediary — for example, an insurance broker.

## Best advice

There is another aspect of the Financial Services Act 1986 which will have an effect on trustees. Investment sales representatives will have to comply with the rules of their regulatory body. In particular, they will have to give best advice and to know their client. This means knowing the client's financial needs and circumstances, including the availability of an occupational scheme. And so the sales representative should get hold of the scheme booklet and learn the main features of the scheme. Otherwise he or she cannot know the client and give best advice. The result is that, in theory at any rate, a member of an occupational scheme should not be able to be seduced into leaving it and taking out a personal pension. The same should also be true for someone who could join but has not yet done so. Often the trustees will learn of the sales representative's approaches. There is no reason why they should not "sell" their scheme; it is not an investment. As long as they stick to comparing occupational schemes and personal schemes, and pointing out the advantages of the company scheme, they need not fear the Financial Services Act. They must not, however, comment or advise on the particular personal pension product.

A great deal of nonsense is talked about the effect of the Financial Services Act on pension scheme trustees. It does not stop them from doing their job of looking after their members or of giving them advice about the choices open to them. The only thing they must not do is give advice about a particular investment product.

For an illustration of the way the Financial Services Act works in practice, readers are referred to "The Lawyer's Tale — A Question of Rank" which follows this chapter.

# The Lawyer's Tale:
# A Question of Rank

Monty Murgatroyd, the Chief General Manager of Magnificent Mutual Life Assurance, was in an irascible mood. The new business figures were poor and the staff were getting lax. At the summer staff dance a visitor, surveying the crowded floor, had asked him how many people worked for the company. "Only one or two," he had replied testily, "the others just come to the office to draw their pay and rest up for their free time activities."

And so he had instituted a crackdown; the superintendents were berated for their excessive expense accounts and daily client visits were banned.

Not that Murgatroyd was against visiting clients. On the contrary, what with the introduction of personal pensions, it was more necessary than ever to visit clients regularly and give presentations about the effects of the new pensions regime.

"But let the young ones have a chance," he continued. "Let's have some fresh blood on the scene. Some of you are looking decidedly jaded. A few months confined to your desks, deprived of high cholesterol lunches, will do you a power of good."

An exception to the rule was Larry Robinson, the new business manager. Soon after the ban Larry was out visiting a company with Sarah Potts, the pensions administrator who actually ran the scheme, and young David who helped Archie Smithers run the documents department.

They were visiting Colonel Braithwaite, who was the managing director of United Widgets.

As an old military man, the Colonel ran his company like a regiment. He knew Sarah and she was just introducing David when Larry joined them. Unfortunately the Colonel took Larry for the chauffeur, perhaps because of his vast cigar.

The Colonel bristled ominously: "Put out that cigar and wait outside. You obviously don't know that smoking is not permitted in my presence. In any event, drivers wait in their vehicles until they are wanted."

Larry backed out scarlet with rage but was afraid to take on an important client like Colonel Braithwaite. Sarah managed to control her giggles and she and David were introduced to the other two trustees; Miss Mather, the Colonel's confidential secretary who in fact ran the company and Ron Taylor, the company's accountant who was absolutely terrified of his employer.

"Before we get on to personal pensions," began the Colonel, "I read an article in the Financial Times about some new Act which says I can't invest my money as I want to. If this journalist johnny is right, I have got to go cap in hand to some investment manager before I can invest the pension fund's cash."

Unlike Larry, David was not frightened by the Colonel.

"There is a difference between investing your own money and that of the pension fund," he said.

"It's all the same to me," interrupted the Colonel. "It's all mine."

Sensibly David let this pass, and continued: "The Financial Services Act regulates investment management and requires registration of investment managers. It will be a criminal offence for trustees to be responsible for investment unless they register with the Investment Management Regulatory Organisation — IMRO. That will mean filling in a long and complicated form and proving that you are a fit and proper person to invest other people's money. What's more you will have to pay a hefty annual fee to IMRO plus a contribution to their compensation fund."

"Goodness gracious me," shouted the Colonel, "where do you get all this bureaucratic gobbledygook from? Are you sure you've got it right? I remember Archie Smithers lecturing me at great length about the trustees' investment duties."

"Times have changed Colonel," said David bravely. "Archie was of course right, but the effect of the Act is, curiously, to deprive trustees of one of their main duties — investment — unless they go through the hoop of registering with IMRO. But pension fund trustees who are not responsible for day to day investment management will not need to register — provided they delegate investment management to someone who is either registered or exempt.

"So it all turns on what is meant by 'day to day investment management'. Luckily the Securities and Investments Board has produced a guide for trustees. While it does not have any legal effect, it does give much useful advice on this point."

"Well, well," said the Colonel admiringly, "you'd better tell us all a bit more about this latest piece of Government interference."

"Day to day investment management is not defined in the Act," continued David smiling, "but the SIB memorandum and speeches by Government Ministers have shed some light.

"There are some areas where trustees can have their say without being in charge of day to day investment management:

— portfolio weighting — the balance between income and capital — what proportion you invest overseas — you can decide all that sort of thing without falling foul of the Act;

— strategic decisions — this overlaps portfolio weighting, but is about how much you put into equities, how much into gilts — that sort of thing;

— decisions not to invest in certain areas; for example, South Africa or tobacco shares."

At this point Miss Mather burst in:

"Oh good, we can stop the brokers investing in those dreadful companies that experiment on animals."

Not to be outdone Ron Taylor piped up:

"We'll be able to decide not to invest in South Africa."

"Stop blithering, you two," said the Colonel. "Let's get on with it. It will soon be noon and my system needs its first gin injection then."

"I'll try to be quick," said David. "You can also reserve the right to decide about sensitive matters like takeovers — not just of the company but others in the industry. You might want to help or hinder the takeover of a competitor. That will not count as day to day investment."

"So apart from these cases," said the Colonel, "my investment adviser rules OK? It's certainly not OK by me — I give the orders to the brokers. I pay the advisers — not the other way round. They do what I tell them. And since that's that, we'll just have five minutes to learn all about personal pensions."

"Well, sir," said David, "perhaps Sarah could have her innings now and tell you about personal pensions and buy-out policies." "Capital," said the Colonel, "I must say I like dealing with you two better than that Mediterranean lounge lizard you brought with you."

"Right," said Sarah. "First of all, trustees can advise about the merits of their own company scheme as opposed to a personal pension. As long as you don't advise on the merits of particular personal pensions and just confine yourself to general advice, then you won't be caught by the Act. Likewise with buy-out policies. You can advise employees about the options open to them when they leave — deferred pension, transfer or a s.32 policy — but not about the merits of rival insurance company products."

"Well, that's your department, Miss Mather," said the Colonel. "You sort out all the troublemakers. If they want a personal pension rather than the company scheme, more fools them. I wouldn't try and stop them. If they want to leave a good job here and try their luck elsewhere, then as far as I am concerned they are defectors and I wouldn't waste words on them — let alone advice."

Sarah smiled sweetly and blew away the Colonel's wrath. "Perhaps I should just finish," she said, "by explaining that a member's rights under an occupational scheme are not 'investments' as defined in the Act, whereas a member's rights under a personal pension are classified as 'investments' unless the underlying investment is cash; for instance, a cash deposit arrangement with a bank or building society. That is because the Act does not regulate deposit accounts with banks and societies."

"Well, that is all very interesting, I am sure," said the Colonel. "But the bar beckons. You will of course stay for lunch. Your chauffeur chappy can take himself down to the local for a sandwich."

Later that afternoon, after an excellent lunch, followed by a frosty drive back to the office with the furious Larry, Sarah and David met up with Archie Smithers.

"I say," he said, "you two went down well with the Colonel. He's been on the telephone to say how marvellous you both were. I must admit I was surprised about his cavalier attitude to employees who opt for a personal pension. But I am not sure we pensions people don't over-egg the pudding sometimes. There will be plenty of employers like the Colonel who will simply say that if you don't know a good thing when you see it, that's up to you. Don't forget they will save money with such people.

"In any event members should not be seduced into leaving a good company scheme for a personal pension without the trustees being forewarned and having a chance to sell their scheme. Insurance salesmen will have to comply with the Conduct of Business Rules and will be under a duty to give best advice for their client's needs. In other words, they would need to know the main features of their client's occupational scheme before they could compare it with a personal pension. I don't really think that a lot of people will opt out of a good company scheme.

But equally if we don't want that to happen, we must take trouble to advertise its virtues and not leave all the running to the personal pensions salesmen. But enough of all that; otherwise I will begin to rival the Colonel for verbosity".

First published in *Pensions Management*, October 1987.

# CHAPTER 8

# Disclosure

## The Disclosure Regulations

The Disclosure of Information Regulations require trustees of occupational pension schemes to disclose certain information about the scheme to the members and other people within certain time limits. The regulations do not apply to schemes with one member or to schemes which provide only death in service benefits. The information that has to be disclosed will seem a little daunting but it will be more digestible if it is broken down under a number of different headings.

### Types of information to be disclosed

A brief outline of the requirements may be helpful. There are five basic types of information:

(a) *The constitution of the scheme*
   Here the information only has to be made available — not given automatically.

(b) *Basic scheme information*
   Here the information has to be given automatically within 13 weeks of the member joining.

(c) *Information for individuals*
   Here the information has to be given automatically on a triggering event; for example, when a benefit becomes payable, or on a member's death, or when a member leaves. Otherwise it only has to be made available on request.

(d) *Scheme winding up*
   Here the information has to be given when winding up commences and when the assets have been realised.

(e) *Trustees' report, accounts, auditor's report, actuarial valuation and statement*
   Here, rather surprisingly, the information only has to be made

available — not supplied automatically.

## Money purchase schemes

In the case of money purchase schemes annual benefit statements must be given automatically. An option statement about the member's protected rights has to be given automatically, normally at state pension age. If a contracted-out money purchase scheme ceases to be contracted-out, the members must be told automatically and they must also be given automatically certain information about their protected rights.

# The constitution of the scheme

### What information has to be disclosed?

Copies of all trust deeds, rules and deeds of amendment, including the names and addresses of all participating employers.

### Who is entitled to the information?

(a)    Members and prospective members (people entitled to join in the future).
(b)    Spouses of members and prospective members.
(c)    Beneficiaries under the scheme (other than members).
(d)    Recognised trade unions but only if the information is relevant to their members.

### How is the information to be given?

By allowing those entitled to inspect copies free of charge within a reasonable time at a reasonable place. Copy documents must be supplied, if asked for, on payment of a reasonable fee.

### When is the information to be given?

On written request but such a request cannot be made more than once every 12 months.

# Basic information about the scheme

What information has to be disclosed?
(a)   Who is eligible to join and the conditions of membership.
(b)   How members' contributions are calculated.
(c)   How employers' contributions are calculated.
(d)   Whether the scheme is tax-approved; if not, whether an application for this is before the Revenue.
(e)   Whether any relevant employment is or is not contracted out.
(f)   What benefits are payable and how they are calculated.
(g)   The conditions on which benefits are paid.
(h)   Which benefits are discretionary.
(i)   Which benefits are funded and which not.
(j)   Which benefits are provided by earmarked insurance policies.
(k)   Whether and to what extent the employer is obliged to pay benefits if the scheme's resources are not sufficient.
(l)   Whether there is power to increase pensions in payment; who can exercise it and whether it is discretionary, including details of the percentage increases during the past scheme year to pensions in payment and deferred pensions with a statement about the extent to which the increases were discretionary. If there have been different increases for different individuals, the maximum, minimum and average percentage increases must be given.
(m)   What provisions there are for refunds of contributions and preservation of benefits for early leavers.
(n)   The name and address for enquiries.
(o)   The period of notice, if any, which a member must give to opt out of the scheme, while remaining in service.
(p)   Whether, and, if so, on what conditions an employee may rejoin the scheme.
(q)   Whether those who are eligible to join are admitted only by application, or automatically unless the person elects not to be admitted.
(r)   Whether information about the scheme has been given to the Registrar of Pension Schemes.
(s)   Whether the scheme falls within the jurisdiction of the Pensions Ombudsman.

(t)    The circumstances in which the Occupational Pensions Advisory Service may assist members of the scheme.

When any of this information is provided, there has also to be a
statement that further information about the scheme is available, giving
the address for enquiries.

### Who is entitled to the information?

(a)    Members and prospective members.
(b)    Spouses of members and prospective members.
(c)    Beneficiaries under the scheme (other than members).
(d)    Recognised trade unions, but only if the information is relevant
to their members.

### How is the information to be given?

Information should be given in writing. Members and beneficiaries have
to be notified of any material change about the name and address for
enquiries within one month. Other material changes must be drawn
to the attention of members, whenever it is practicable, before they
take effect; and otherwise within one month of the change.

### When is the information to be given?

Information must be given automatically to everyone who becomes a
member within 13 weeks of joining. This is one of the rare cases where
information has to be given without any request. On receipt of a written
request information must be given within one month in other cases,
but such a request cannot be made more than once every three years.

# Information for individuals — what has to be disclosed?

### Benefit statements

These should include the following:

(a)    The amount of benefit payable.
(b)    If a benefit is payable periodically, the conditions on which

payment will be continued and the provisions (if any) under which the amount payable will be altered.
(c) At the trustees' choice either —
(i) the amount of the member's own benefits and of his or her survivors' benefits payable from normal pension age or later death, calculated as if his or her service ended within one month of the date of the statement, without regard to future salary increases; or
(ii) the amount of the member's own benefits and of his or her survivors' benefits payable from normal pension age or later death, calculated as if his or her service were to continue to normal pension age without regard to future salary increases; or
(iii) the method by which these amounts may be calculated, with enough information about past salaries and service to enable the calculation to be made.

This information must be given automatically when a benefit becomes payable or within one month afterwards. When the amount of a benefit is about to be altered, the beneficiary must be told before or within one month afterwards.

Even before a benefit becomes payable or is altered, a member can ask the trustees for a benefit statement and they must comply within two months. But the member cannot do this more than once a year and the requirement does not apply to money purchase benefits.

## Statements about death benefits and options

The following must be disclosed:
(a) the rights and options available on the death of a member or beneficiary;
(b) the provisions (or a statement that there are none) under which survivors' benefits may or will be increased, and whether such increases are discretionary.

The information must be given automatically when a member or beneficiary dies, as soon as possible after the death, to anyone over 18 who has rights under the scheme, so long as the trustees know his or her address. The information must also be given on request within two months to a personal representative or someone authorised to act on behalf of the person entitled to the rights. Such a request cannot be made more than once every three years.

## Early leaver statements

The following information must be provided:
(a)   The rights and options available to an early leaver. This informa-
      tion must be given within two months after the member's
      request, but he or she cannot make such a request more than
      once a year. In addition, the information must be given
      automatically within two months after the trustees are told
      that his or her service is to end.
(b)   Whether any transfer value is or would be available; and if so —
      (i)    an estimate of its amount;
      (ii)   the rights to which it relates;
      (iii)  whether any part is attributable to additional benefits
             awarded at the trustees' discretion;
      (iv)   if the estimated amount is less than the statutory norm,
             this must be explained plus the estimated date for giving
             the full amount, and the member must be told of his or her
             right to get further estimates.
This information must be given within two months after the
member's request, but he or she cannot make such a request more
than once a year.
      (v)    Whether a contribution refund is or would be available,
             and in what circumstances, with an estimate of the amount
             and an explanation of the method of calculation.
This information must be given within two months after the
member's request, but he or she cannot make such a request more
than once a year. The obligation does not apply if the information has
already been given and all the contributions were before April 1975 or
he or she had been told that no refund was available.

## Statements about transfer credits

A member must be told if the scheme will accept a transfer payment
from another scheme and, if so, the amount of the transfer credit. The
information must be given as soon as possible on written request but
such a request cannot be made more than once a year.
    When any information is given to individuals, they have to be told
that further information is available, giving the address for enquiries.

## Statements about bulk transfers

Where it is proposed that a bulk transfer of members' rights to another occupational pension scheme takes place without the members' consent, information about the transfer must be given one month before the transfer takes place.

## Independent trustees

Members must be told whether an independent trustee has been appointed where the employer is insolvent.

## Winding up the scheme

When trustees start to wind up a scheme, they must automatically and within one month inform all members and beneficiaries. After the assets have been realised and after they have been applied under the winding up rule, they must automatically and within two months —

(a) Inform every member and beneficiary of the amount of benefit payable.

(b) If a benefit is payable periodically, the conditions on which the payment will be continued, and the provisions (if any) under which the amount payable will be altered.

(c) Inform every member of the amount of his or her and of his or her survivors' benefits payable from normal pension age or later death. Alternatively the trustees can specify the method by which these amounts can be calculated with enough information about past service and salaries to enable the calculation to be made. This requirement does not apply to money purchase benefits.

(d) Inform every member and beneficiary whether, and, if so, by how much, the benefits are reduced because of insufficient resources.

(e) Who will be liable to pay the benefits after winding up.

(f) The address for enquiries about entitlement to benefits after the scheme is wound up.

# CHAPTER 9

# Accounts and Trustees' Reports

## Audited accounts

Audited accounts must be prepared for each scheme year. An auditor must be qualified and cannot be a scheme member, trustee, an employee of the trustees, one of the employers, or a director or employee of one of the employers or one of its connected companies.

### What the accounts must contain

(a) An account of the financial additions to and withdrawals from the fund during the scheme year.

(b) A statement of the assets at market value (or the trustees' estimate where the market value is not easily come by) and the liabilities of the scheme (other than liabilities to pay benefits after the end of the scheme year). If the value of any assets is estimated, the reason why must be given. The asset statement must show the distribution of investments between each of the following categories:

(i) insurance policies;
(ii) public sector fixed interest investments;
(iii) other fixed interest investments;
(iv) index-linked securities;
(v) equities;
(vi) property;
(vii) property unit trusts;
(viii) other unit trusts;
(ix) property managed funds;
(x) other managed funds;
(xi) loans;
(xii) cash deposits;
(xiii) other investments.

Each category must show separately United Kingdom and overseas investments and must state, in the case of unit trusts and managed funds, whether the managers are United Kingdom registered or not.

(c)    A reconciliation of the income and expenditure account with the statement of assets and liabilities.

(d)    In the case of non-sterling assets or liabilities, the sterling equivalent with the basis of conversion.

(e)    Details of any investment comprising more than 5% of the scheme's assets.

(f)    A statement of the proportion of the scheme's assets invested in employer-related investments, and where that exceeds 5%, the steps being taken to reduce it to 5%.

(g)    For every amount shown in the accounts, a statement of the corresponding amount for the previous year.

(h)    The total of purchases and sales of investments in the scheme year.

(i)    A statement about whether the accounts have been prepared in accordance with the current Statement of Recommended Practice No. 1 Pension Scheme Accounts (SORP1) with details of any significant departures.

## True and fair view

The accounts must also show a true and fair view of the financial transactions of the scheme and of the disposition of the assets and liabilities. Liabilities to pay benefits after the end of the scheme year do not have to be included. The accounts must also contain the auditor's report.

## The auditor's report

The auditor's report must say:

(a)    whether or not the statutory requirements are satisfied;

(b)    whether or not contributions have been paid in accordance with the rules and the actuary's recommendation;

(c)    if either or both of these statements are negative or qualified, the reasons why.

# Actuarial valuation and statement

## What they must contain

The trustees have to obtain an actuarial valuation of the scheme's assets in relation to its liabilities. This must:

(a)    enable the expected future course of the contribution rates and funding level to be understood;

(b)    state whether it has been prepared in accordance with current professional guidelines;

(c)    indicate whether there are any significant departures from these guidelines.

An actuarial valuation is not required for public sector schemes, unfunded schemes, money purchase schemes and schemes where the benefits are provided by earmarked insurance policies.

## Time limits

The first valuation has to be obtained three and a half years from the scheme's start date.

Subsequent valuations must not be later than three and a half years from the previous one.

## The actuarial statement

Each valuation must be accompanied by a statement describing:

(a)    the effective date of valuation;

(b)    the security of accrued rights — whether the assets fully cover the liabilities;

(c)    the measures to be taken to bring these to 100% and the expected date of achievement;

(d)    the security of prospective rights — whether the scheme resources are likely to meet in full liabilities as they fall due;

(e)    a summary of the methods and assumptions used.

# The trustees' report

The annual trustees' report has to contain:

(a)    The latest audited accounts.

(b)    The latest actuarial statement.

(c)    The names of the trustees, and whether they have access to a copy of the statement on the principles of pension scheme trusteeship issued by the Occupational Pensions Board.

(d)  The provisions for appointing and removing trustees.

(e)  The names of the actuaries, auditors, solicitors, banks and other persons retained by the trustees with details of any changes since the previous year.

(f)  The address for enquiries about the scheme or benefits.

(g)  Any changes since the previous year in the basic information about the scheme given to members or prospective members.

(h)  The number of members and beneficiaries at any one date during the year.

(i)  The percentage increases made during the year to pensions and deferred pensions, with a statement about whether the increases were discretionary, and, if so, to what extent. If there have been different increases for different individuals or groups, the maximum, minimum and average percentage increases must be given.

(j)  A statement about whether any transfer values paid during the year were calculated in the prescribed way, whether they were less than the statutory norm, and, if so, why, and when full values are likely to be available.

(k)  Whether the trustees will accept cash equivalents and provide transfer credits.

(l)  Whether the trustees have directed that any cash equivalent shall not be increased to take account of discretionary pension increases or similar benefits.

(m)  If the auditor's statement shows any discrepancy about contributions, the reasons must be given and when it is likely to be resolved.

(n)  If any such discrepancy was left unresolved in a previous year, how it is likely to be resolved.

(o)  A review by the trustees of the financial development of the scheme during the year and its financial prospects.

(p)  Who has managed the investments and the extent of any delegation of investment management.

(q)  The basis on which the investment manager is paid and how any fee or commission is calculated, if the scheme bears these costs.

(r)  An investment report containing —

(i)  A statement by the trustees or the investment manager of the scheme's investment policies and any significant change;

(ii)   A review of investment performance during the year and the nature, disposition, marketability, security and valuation of the scheme's assets.

(s)   The scheme's auditor's resignation statement. Where an auditor resigns or is removed, he or she must state whether there are any circumstances connected with his or her resignation or removal significantly affecting members' interests, or that he or she knows of no such circumstances.

# Availability of audited accounts, actuarial valuations, statements and trustees' reports

### Who is entitled to the information?

The following are entitled to the information:
(a)   members and prospective members (people entitled to join in the future);
(b)   beneficiaries;
(c)   recognised trade unions with members in the scheme.

### How is the information to be given?

The information is given by allowing those entitled on request to inspect copies free of charge within a reasonable time at a reasonable place. Copies of the latest document must be supplied (but only once), if requested, free of charge within one month. Such a request cannot be made more than once every three years in the case of an actuarial valuation and a copying charge is allowed for actuarial valuations. The trustees must take reasonable steps to draw attention to the availability of these documents within one month of their becoming available. When any of these documents are supplied, there must be a written statement that further information about the scheme is available, giving the address for enquiries.

### When is the information to be given?

Information should be given not later than one year after each scheme year, but in the case of an actuarial valuation within three months after the trustees receive a written request.

## Scheme year

A scheme year is one of the following periods selected by the trustees:
 (a)   a year specified for the purpose in the trust deed or rules;
 (b)   a calendar year;
 (c)   the 12 months ending 31 March, or
        the 12 months ending 5 April.
Where the trustees fail to select a scheme year, it means a period of 12 months beginning on 1st April.

# Money purchase schemes

The regulations have imposed certain additional requirements for money purchase schemes.

### Annual benefit statements

A member of a money purchase scheme must receive an annual benefit statement, whether or not he or she asks for it. This statement must show:
 (a)   the amount of contributions credited to the member in the previous 12 months, and, if the scheme is contracted out, how much was attributable to the contracting out rebate and how much to the 2% incentive;
 (b)   the value of the member's protected rights and the value of the member's rights (other than protected rights);
 (c)   if the value of the member's transfer value rights payable on leaving the scheme is less than the value of the member's total rights under the scheme, the difference must be shown. This relates, for example, to an insurance policy surrender penalty.

### Option statements

A member who has protected rights must be told of his or her options for all his or her accrued rights (not just protected rights) under the scheme not less than four but more than six months before state pension age (65 for a man or 60 for a woman).
 The duty of disclosure does not apply in certain cases:
 (a)   to any person whose benefits have been extinguished;
 (b)   to any member or prospective member if the trustees have not been told about him or her;
 (c)   to a recognised trade union if the trustees have not been told about it.
 Readers are referred to "The Duty to Tell", which follows this chapter, for an illustration of how certain disclosure problems can be resolved.

# The Lawyer's Tale:
# The Duty to Tell

Maurice Meredith, a fussy little man with a bow tie, was the company secretary at Anglo-Consolidated Investments in the City. It was a smallish investment management house with about 30 employees and a good final salary pension scheme. He had spent an enjoyable Saturday morning reading the *Financial Times* as was his routine. He explained to his wife that it was a very necessary part of his work and that he must never be disturbed unless, of course, the chairman rang. Mrs Meredith guessed the truth — that it was all an elaborate charade designed to avoid his having to go shopping with her.

This particular Saturday Meredith got a shock. He had read an article on the new disclosure regulations. They were going to force pension trustees to reveal all sorts of things that in a well regulated company remained hidden from public gaze. The author was saying that copies of all the trust deeds and rules had to be given on request to members and that if a scheme provided different benefits for different classes of employees, that would now be brought out into the open. Alternatively there would have to be a separate scheme set up for the members with different benefits. It was this that had given him such a shock.

Anglo-Consolidated's pension scheme was with the Magnificent Mutual and was one of the jewels in its crown. There were not all that many members but they were all highly paid, and the total contributions each year were astronomical. There was the usual benefit structure that one would expect from a good scheme, but in the case of one or two members, better benefits had been promised. The favoured few, namely the chairman and a couple of directors, got an accrual rate of 30ths instead of 60ths, four times (instead of twice) salary lump sum death benefits and ⅔, instead of ½, widow's pensions. Recently Meredith had been elevated to the category of senior executive. He knew how strongly the chairman felt about the confidentiality of the arrangements and how upset he would be if they came out.

Meredith's pleasant Saturday routine therefore received a very unpleasant jolt. He immediately telephoned the chairman, Sir Lancelot Chrimes. Sir Lancelot had a very simplistic view of life, which probably explained why he had made so much money in the City. He listened tolerantly to Meredith's prediction of trouble and said "Look here, Meredith, you and I don't waste our time on worries like that. There is always a way round these problems. Get on to the lawyers on Monday and tell them to come up with a solution."

Meredith sighed. Anglo-Consolidated's lawyers, Sue, Grabbit and Run, were a smallish City firm. They were good commercial lawyers but knew nothing about pensions. This was one of the attractions of the Magnificent Mutual so far as Meredith was concerned. Pensions were their business. John Watson, the pensions superintendent, who looked after the Anglo-Consolidated scheme, was calm, competent and capable. In his care the scheme ran like clockwork. Meredith knew from bitter experience, as did Watson, what a meal the lawyers had made of the draft trust deed and rules which the Magnificent Mutual had produced for the scheme. Meredith would rather have consulted John Watson about the problem. But when Sir Lancelot spoke, he expected his orders to be carried out.

Meredith duly rang the lawyers on Monday morning and explained the problem. The partner admitted that he was not au fait with the regulations but would look into the matter. Meredith correctly surmised that he had never even heard of them; he often thought they got far better value from their subscription to the *Financial Times* than from the vast fees they paid to their lawyers.

A week later Sir Lancelot asked for a progress report. Nothing had happened reported Meredith. He was promptly told to chase the lawyers. Emboldened by this Meredith asked if he might consult John Watson about the problem. After all pensions were his business.

"Capital idea," said Sir Lancelot, "Why didn't you do it before? We get their advice for nothing. You can't expect me to have to tell you everything. I have the responsibility for running the company — details are for you, Meredith."

This was a typical stroke of Sir Lancelot's genius for latching on to other people's ideas and promptly claiming them as his own. So Meredith phoned Watson and asked him to come and see him to advise on how to get out of the difficulty.

John of course knew all about the disclosure regulations. Archibald Smithers, the Magnificent Mutual's in-house lawyer, had provided the superintendents with a comprehensive briefing on the subject. Smithers had recently taken a grip on himself after his recent shortcomings, bought a new suit, got his hair cut and received old Murgatroyd's permission to hire an assistant.

The assistant was a cleancut fresh faced young man called David. He had gently and tactfully reorganised Smithers, taking over much of his documentation work, thus leaving him free to get up to date and give the advisory service to the superintendents which he had so signally neglected.

John sought out Smithers to consult him about the problem. He found him with Larry Robinson, the Magnificent Mutual's brash new business manager. Even the born again Smithers looked dowdy and down at heel compared with Larry with his animal vitality bursting forth in his fashionable light grey suit and black suede shoes. This was all part of Larry's new youthful go-go image. Luckily, Larry was just leaving and so John was relieved that he would not have to pour oil on the usually stormy waters of the relationship between the two men.

Smithers immediately asked John how these additional benefits in the Anglo-Consolidated scheme were granted — was it by individual letters or were they spelt out in the booklet and in the rules.

"Oh no," said John "there are so few involved that we just prepare individual benefit letters for signature by the trustees."

"That's all right then" said Smithers. "It's only booklets, trust deeds and rules that have to be available as of right to all members, their spouses, other beneficiaries and trade unions. Not individual letters like these, because they don't affect the members generally. You won't therefore have the hassle of setting up a new scheme for the senior executives."

"What a relief that will be for Meredith" said John. "While I'm here, can you bone me up on any other features of the regulations that I should be telling him about."

"Certainly," said Smithers, "but wouldn't you like me to come along with you to the meeting?"

"No, no" said John a little too quickly. "That won't be necessary." Why was there such a reluctance, thought Smithers huffily, to let docs people, as they were called in the industry, come out of their closets? He didn't after all have two heads. Docs people were expected to be neither seen nor heard — one worse than small children. Oh well, Smithers sighed, here goes.

"We have already discussed the requirement to disclose the constitution of the scheme, the trust deeds and rules and any amending deeds. The law also requires basic information about the scheme to be given automatically to members, beneficiaries and trade unions. This is more or less the old Revenue requirement of communicating the essential features of a scheme and is usually done through a scheme booklet. However beneficiaries, such as spouses, and trade unions now have a legal right to the information.

"Probably the only two items of information not normally in a booklet are the requirement to say if and to what extent the employer is obliged to pay up if the scheme is insolvent; and the requirement to state whether there is power to increase pensions and whether it is discretionary."

"Some employers are not going to like that, Archie" said John, "plus it's going to worry some members if they're told their employer does not have to make good any deficiency."

"Well, there it is," said Archie "that is what the regulations say." They then went through the requirements about individual benefit statements and the new trustees' report and its accompanying audited accounts and auditor's and actuarial statements.

A few days later John Watson presented himself at the offices of the Anglo-Consolidated. He sat down with Meredith and gave him the good news about the senior executives' benefits. For good measure he relayed the advice given to him by Smithers about the new requirements.

The totally new obligation was, of course, the annual trustees' report. He explained that this had got to contain:

— the names of the trustees and the rules for appointing and removing them;
— names of the actuaries, auditors, solicitors and bankers (there was a nice free plug for the professionals, thought Meredith);
— the numbers of members;
— percentage increases made voluntarily to pensions and deferred pensions, whether they were discretionary; and if there had been different increases for different individuals or groups, the maximum, minimum and average increases must be given.

At that point, Meredith, whose eyes had been beginning to glaze over, sat up and said "We will have to watch that one carefully when Sir Lancelot retires . . ."

"You won't get out of that quite so easily as you have with your senior executives' letters," said John. "Some schemes will either have to change their ways or publish what they have done. Meredith blanched but recognised that that problem was not for this year.

John concluded: the report will also have to include:

— a financial review of the year;
— details of the investment managers;
— how the investment managers are paid;
— an investment report including performance.

"That could be embarrassing if we don't perform well" said Meredith. The Magnificent Mutual had been forced to delegate investment management to the Anglo-Consolidated as the price for getting the scheme.

"Curiously enough" said John "although Parliament requires all this information to be published for members, it only has to be available. In other words it does not have to be sent out to the members. But the trustees do have to take reasonable steps to draw attention to the availability of the report and its accompanying actuarial and auditor's statements."

During this recital the office clock had ticked on to the magic hour of 12.30. "If you've finished" said Meredith courteously "will you be good enough to meet Sir Lancelot for a pre-lunch drink and then have lunch with me in the directors' dining room. I am sure Sir Lancelot will be delighted to hear your advice."

A few minutes later John had in his hand one of the traditional City pint-sized gin and tonics and was telling the good news to the chairman. "Capital, capital" he said. "Horses for courses, Meredith. No use going to Sue, Grabbit and Run about a thing like this. Lawyers don't know about pensions. Told you to consult young Watson in the first place."

Meredith knew his chairman well enough to take this for the compliment it was meant to be. But honest John Watson began to go red. "I have taken the advice of our own lawyer about this. He is an expert in the field. Indeed he is a member of the Association of Pension Lawyers. Pensions law is very specialised and it would be unwise to consult a lawyer who didn't have an intimate knowledge of the subject.'

"Quite right. As I said, horses for courses. You don't go to a butcher to cut out your appendix. Your candour does you credit, young man. And now, if you will excuse me, I must be off to lunch with our brokers. Look after our visitor well, Meredith."

The moral, John mused later that day, was that Smithers was right. Trustees and employers would have to have more of an eye on the audience. They would have to be careful about discretionary benefits. But if all this expensively produced information just ended up in the bin, like so many company reports, what was the point of it all?

John instinctively grasped this. His conclusion was that while yet another load of bumph was going to have to be produced by the hard pressed pension administrators, it was unlikely that the members would be much better off as a result.

First published in *Pensions Management*, November 1986.

*CHAPTER 10*

# Delegation, Conflict and Disagreement

## Delegation

Trustees are given wide powers by the Trustee Act 1925 and by the scheme rules to delegate certain of their powers and duties. Nevertheless they remain in control. Principal areas of delegation are the appointment of a secretary, actuary, auditor, solicitor, bank and investment manager.

## Choosing agents

Trustees can pay their agents reasonable remuneration for their services and they must exercise care in selecting and choosing them. As long as they do this, and exercise a reasonable degree of supervision, they will not be responsible for the agent's acts or defaults.

## Rules of delegation

The way in which investment management is delegated has been dealt with in Chapters 6 and 7. Sometimes trustees delegate certain discretionary powers, like paying lump sum death in service benefits, to a committee or to local managers or committees. If the rules do not authorise this, the trustees will remain responsible for the acts of their delegates. And so scheme rules commonly set out extensive powers of delegation by trustees and authorise them to appoint committees to deal with certain matters. They often also deal fully with the appointment, payment and removal of agents such as actuaries. The reason for this is not to bestow these powers (this has already been conferred by the Trustee Act) but to make it clear who has the power. Often the right to

appoint and remove the actuary, for example, is not given solely to the
trustees; it may be given to the employer and in other cases it is a power
to be exercised by the employer and the trustees jointly.

## Conflict of interest

Trustees of pension schemes are often directors of the employing company or, at any rate, employees and they will probably be members of
the scheme as well. The rules will probably say that the fact that a trustee
is a member and an employee will not invalidate any decisions taken by
him or her. Even in the absence of such a rule, it is most unlikely that any
action taken by a trustee could be set aside on the grounds of his or her
personal interest.

## Trustees are not negotiators

In exercising their powers and carrying out their duties trustees must
beware of conflicts of interest. When they are acting as trustees of the
pension scheme, they must pay no regard to their other responsibilities,
for example, as trade union officials or directors of the employer. Since
the primary duty of trustees is to administer the scheme in accordance
with the rules, conflicts of interest should not cause problems very often.
Trustees do not usually have a negotiating role and thus it is not usually
part of their duties to seek benefit improvements or contribution holidays for their members. If, faced with a conflict, a trustee is in doubt
about what to do, he or she can either abstain or else seek professional
advice. Trustees should also consult their members in appropriate cases.

## Disagreement

The law requires trustees to act unanimously unless the rules allow
them to act by a majority. Nowadays most pension scheme rules permit
trustees to act by a majority but usually stipulate a quorum or minimum
number necessary for a valid decision. It is generally considered sensible
not to require unanimity because in that situation one trustee could
block the wishes of the others. If a trustee strongly disagrees with the
wishes of the others, the right thing to do is not to seek to veto the
decision, but either to abstain or, in extreme cases, to resign. As in cases

of conflict of interest, a trustee can always seek professional advice and even, in appropriate cases, apply to the court for directions.

Readers are referred to "The Lawyers Tale — Splitting the Apple", which follows this chapter, for an illustration of how such problems may be resolved.

# The Lawyer's Tale: Splitting the Apple

It had been a bad morning for Colin Bell, the deputy pensions actuary at the Magnificent Mutual Life Assurance Society. He had been asked to produce costings for deferred pensions for the members on the winding up of the Cox's Orange Pension Scheme. No one likes winding up pension schemes, least of all insurance companies. It is a scheme lost, not a scheme gained. He got his assistant John Tomkins to work out the figures. As an actuary, Colin would not, of course, dirty his own hands with menial work like that. What emerged was that the cost of buying out the benefits was of the order of £700,000. That left a surplus of about £900,000. Under the winding up rule the trustees had discretion to augment benefits up to Revenue limits. Anything left over had to be paid back to the company.

What was disturbing both Colin and John was that the company, Cox's Orange, had just been taken over by a French firm, based in Normandy, called Golden Delicious. It was they who had instigated the winding up of the scheme.

"We'll have to write to the trustees giving them the figures and give them various costings for benefit improvements to mop up the surplus. We'd better suggest we go and see them to discuss it all," said Colin.

"That would be excellent," said John. "Their head office is in Rouen. We will go on a Thursday and come back the following Monday."

A letter was duly despatched to Rouen. A week later a curt reply was received. It announced that Golden Delicious had removed the old trustees of the pension scheme and substituted two Golden Delicious employees in their place. Furthermore, a copy of the deed in faultless legal English was enclosed. The letter went on to instruct the Magnificent Mutual to buy out the members' benefits with deferred annuity policies and to pay a cheque for the balance to the company. In the same post came a letter of complaint from one of the trustees who had been so summarily replaced.

"Well there goes our weekend in Normandy," said Colin to John when he showed him the two letters.

"I don't like this, and Philip will like it even less." Philip was the senior pensions actuary and was Colin's and John's boss. "You know how he hates any kind of complaint."

"But it isn't a complaint about the Magnificent Mutual," replied John. "It's not our fault. We've just got to do what we're told."

"I'm going to have a word with Archie Smithers. I feel a touch of the wobblies about this," said Colin. Archie was the Society's lawyer who ran the documents department. He and Colin were old friends.

So off he went in search of Archie. And as so often he failed to find him. Nor did he find young David, Archie's assistant. He was away on holiday. He did, however, manage to track down Sylvia, their secretary, and Matthew, the latest recruit to the docs department. Matthew was a newly qualified lawyer who thought he would give pensions a whirl. He was small and earnest and sometimes felt life's burdens weighed heavily upon him.

"Where is the old goat then?" cried Colin. "I don't know why we pay him and Dave. They just set the word processor on autopilot and go away."

"Archie is at a conference and David is on holiday, so I'm in charge of the shop today. You needn't worry about the documents; all is going quite smoothly in their absence," replied Matthew a touch frostily.

Colin gave a great baying laugh. "I know that. Sylvia does the documents - we all know that. It's just that when they're not here, their uselessness becomes embarrassingly obvious."

"Well in that case I'm sure I don't know why you're wasting my time now," snapped Matthew.

"Don't take on so, lad," said Colin jovially. "We don't usually need a pensions lawyer. Some people don't even think they serve any purpose at all."

Poor Matthew was not equipped for this kind of banter. Colin went on: "Read this winding up rule, lad", he said, "plus a couple of letters and tell me if I've got a problem."

After a few minutes, Matthew looked up and said that the new trustees were now in place, the pension scheme was terminated and the trustees had resolved to buy out the members' scale benefits and pay the surplus to the company.

"What you don't seem to have done is to point out to them,"

Matthew continued, "that the repayment of the surplus to the company will attract a free-standing 40% tax charge. Nor have you reminded the trustees that they have a discretion to augment the members' benefits up to Revenue limits. You might also have pointed out to them that the OPB, in its recent report, recommended that on a winding up the members' benefits should be revalued in line with prices, with a limit of 5%."

"Proper little know-all, you are for sure," replied Colin. "Just draft me a reply and I'll fax it through to Rouen."

The fax was sent off and back came a curt reply confirming the previous instructions. Greatly daring, Matthew drafted a further fax for Colin, pointing out that the trustees' duties were to look after their members. They had an unfettered discretion to augment benefits. How could it be in the members' interests to pay over the whole of the surplus to the company?

Back came an even curter fax thanking the Magnificent Mutual for its unsolicited advice. Golden Delicious had taken its own legal advice. The trustees had a discretion; how they exercised it was their affair. They were not accountable to the Magnificent Mutual. A cheque by return was required. To make matters worse, in the same post came a letter from the members who said they were consulting the Occupational Pensions Advisory Service and threatened to take the Magnificent Mutual to court if their benefits were not augmented.

"I've had enough of this," said Colin to Matthew later that day. "We'll have a go at sorting out this mess first thing tomorrow."

And so the next day Colin, John and Matthew sat down in a conference room to brainstorm the problem through.

"I formulated some propositions at home last night," started Matthew. "First, that deed appointing the new trustees is a bit dodgy. If it was signed after the winding up started, it could be invalid as the company's power may cease on winding up. Even if that were not the case, the deed might be set aside as being a misuse of a fiduciary power. A power to appoint and remove trustees can't be exercised to secure some ulterior objective like benefitting the company. It can only be used to further the members' interests."

"Well," said John, " they only put their own stooges in because they wouldn't cause trouble; so the deed is no good then?"

"The problem," replied Matthew, "is proving it."

"You're a real iffy lawyer, aren't you," said Colin. "Get to the point."

"Secondly," continued Matthew, "the trustees — whoever they are

— have got to act in the interests of the members. It's difficult to see how giving the surplus to the company is in the members' interests. In most cases where the trustees have an unfettered discretion, they should use the surplus to augment benefits up to Revenue limits. Only what's left after that should be paid to the company. Of course there may be situations where it would not be right to use all the surplus in that way. It all depends on the facts."

"Get on with it, lad," said Colin testily. "We haven't got all morning."

"Thirdly," went on Matthew, "the exercise by trustees of a discretionary power can only be set aside if it was made for an improper motive, or if they didn't make proper enquiries before reaching their decision, or if their decision is so capricious that no reasonable trustee could have reached it. It's this last ground that looks as if it were the case here."

Colin and John had had enough of this legal monologue. "It's all a matter for the trustees, not us," said Colin. "They've made their decision, right or wrong, and we've got to do as they tell us. If we don't, then whatever we may feel, we'll end up in court."

"Not so fast!" cried Matthew, pink with excitement. "Archie rang me up last night and I checked through these points with him. He added one final proposition.

"As administrators of the scheme the Magnificent Mutual stood in the same position as the trustees themselves. They owe fiduciary duties to the members. They are in the American terminology 'plan fiduciaries'. And so if they did what the trustees ordered, and it was a breach of trust, the Magnificent Mutual would also be in breach and could be ordered to repay the money."

There was an awful silence while this sank in.

"To be safe, we would really have to apply to the court for directions as to how to proceed," said Matthew rubbing his hands gleefully at the prospect.

"It all comes of sending Archie to those foreign pension confer- ences," muttered Colin darkly. "He picks up strange ideas. I knew no good would come of them." With that he rose to his feet, turned on his heels, nearly knocking John down in the process, and they marched out leaving Matthew high and dry.

"How much would it cost," Colin asked John, "to augment the benfits on the lines of the OPB report - RPI indexation with a ceiling of 5%?"

"Oh, about £500,000," said John. "Mind you, that's only a quick approximation."

The following week Archie had returned from his holiday and he and Matthew were summoned to an eight o'clock meeting with Colin and John by Philip, the senior pensions actuary. Apparently he wanted to be put in the frame about the Cox's Orange pension scheme and had an early morning window in his diary.

The meeting started off, after a half hour delay while Philip did his telephone calls, with Colin and John giving their progress report.

"We tracked down the Finance Director of Golden Delicious in Maidstone where the English factory is. So John and I went to see him. We also saw the old trustees and all seven members of the scheme. We got it all sorted out and we then had a long French lunch with wine and Calvados and cigars in the boardroom. We had a lovely day, didn't we John? And what's more we agreed a £50,000 winding up fee for the Magnificent Mutual."

"However did you sort all that out?" asked Archie with a touch of irritation in his voice.

"It was all quite easy," replied Colin. "We told the Finance Director that if he wanted the lot, we'd have to apply to the court for directions. And we told the members that if they wanted the lot, the same thing would happen. A fair old chunk of the surplus would be wasted on the lawyers. So why didn't we act like sensible folk and split it down the middle. So everyone agreed and we all had lunch."

"I am sorry to put a spanner in the works," said Archie, "but if there was a breach of trust, your precious agreement wouldn't rule out a claim by a contingent member such as a spouse."

"Pack it in," said Colin. "I thought you were paid to solve problems - not to invent them!"

"It just goes to prove how right I am about rules," observed Philip. "Everything must be cut and dried. The trustees should never be given unfettered powers. They are only spending someone else's money. The rules should have required the company's consent before they could augment benefits. That way the problem would never have arisen. Thank you, Matthew, for your contribution and congratulations to Colin and John for solving the problem. As for you Archie, just make sure our rules give defined benefits and that trustees never have an unfettered discretion."

First published in *Pensions Management*, December 1989.

# CHAPTER 11

# Merger and Winding Up

## Merger

As a result of takeovers or company reorganisations, an employer may end up with two or more pension schemes. It would save time and money in terms of administration costs if the schemes were merged. Sometimes one person may be a trustee of both the schemes. There are two points to consider:

### *Is a merger authorised?*

Do the rules give the trustees power to bring about a merger? If not, they should be altered so as to facilitate the merger. If the merger is to be effected by a winding up of one of the schemes, no express power in the rules may be necessary.

### *Should the trustees agree to the merger?*

Even if it is authorised, should the trustees agree to the merger? This depends on whether it is in the interests of their members. It must be remembered that for this purpose members include not just active members but also pensioners and those with preserved pensions, who have left the employer's service but retained the right to a pension from the scheme when they retire. Questions of the benefits to be offered by the new scheme and of its solvency will arise. The trustees can only agree to the merger if it is in the interests of the generality of their members and if their rights and expectations in the new scheme are no less favourable overall than their rights and expectations in the old scheme. There must also be enough money in the new scheme, after the merger has taken place, to provide adequate security for the members' rights and expectations. Trustees may have to take account of a surplus or deficit in their own scheme or the new scheme. This will affect the security of their members' benefits.

# Bulk transfers

Bulk transfers of members from one scheme to another should not take place without getting members' individual consents unless the actuary to the transferring scheme certifies that the rights and expectations in the new scheme in respect of past pensionable service are no less favourable overall than such rights and expectations in the old scheme. To avoid members complaining afterwards that the merger was not in their interests, it is often a good idea to get individual consents. Since scheme membership is voluntary, there is not a lot of point in effecting bulk transfers of members without their consent, if they then opt out of the new scheme.

# Winding up

The events which cause a scheme to be wound up are set out in the winding up rule. Sometimes it is a notice from the employer, or the employer's insolvency; sometimes the trustees can decide it is no longer possible to continue the scheme. Often the rule will give the trustees power to continue the scheme as a closed one with no new members and no more employer contributions.

# Surplus on winding up

When an event occurs to trigger a winding up, the assets are realised and applied to secure scheme benefits in the order of priorities set out in the winding up rule. Great care must be taken to apply the assets in the right order and to deal with any surplus that there may be exactly as directed by the rules. If the surplus has to be or is, in the exercise of the trustees' discretion, paid over to the employer, a fixed tax charge of 40% has to be deducted from the payment by the trustees, who must then account for the tax to the Inland Revenue. But before any payment out of the scheme can be made to the employer, all pensions must be guaranteed to increase in line with the rise in the Retail Prices Index with a limit of 5% — LPI or limited price indexation. Trustees may well have a discretion to augment benefits up to Inland Revenue limits, either with or without the employer's consent. Professional advice, especially advice from the actuary, will be needed before deciding how to exercise these powers.

If a final salary scheme has a deficit on winding up, the amount of the deficiency is due from the employer as an ordinary (unsecured) debt. This will not of course do the members much good if the employer is insolvent. If the winding up of the scheme is caused by the employer's insolvency, an independent trustee will have to be appointed. This will avoid the problems caused by the potential conflicts of interest that otherwise might arise. Chapter 20 "Help for the Individual" discusses this in greater detail.

For an illustration of the difficulties that can arise in this area, readers are referred to "The Lawyer's Tale: Throwing Money Away" which follows this chapter.

# The Lawyer's Tale: Throwing Money Away

Ebenezer and Frump was a small firm of solicitors in the City, which was on the skids. They could not compete with the mega law factories, which controlled all the big legal work that was around.

Major Frump, the senior partner, looked a typical solicitor — pince nez glasses and pin stripe suit, a little shiny with excessive wear. He had a Hitler moustache, and a voice like an upper class horse.

One day the telephone rang and he got instructions to sell a company — the Amalgamated Investment Corporation — for £150,000. By Frump's standards that was a big job. The company had a pension scheme administered by the Magnificent Mutual Life Assurance Society. His client told him the pension scheme had a substantial surplus and that he should get advice from the Magnificent Mutual to ensure that the buyer did not get the benefit of it for nothing.

This threw Frump. He knew nothing at all about pension schemes nor very much about company acquisitions come to that. He rang John Watson, the pensions superintendent who looked after the scheme, and fixed a meeting with him and Sir Lancelot Chrimes, the owner of Amalgamated Investment, for the following day. John brought with him to the meeting his deputy Belinda.

Belinda had boned up on the problem before the meeting so John set her to work. She opened up with her blockbusting smile and promptly had Sir Lancelot eating out of her hand.

"Pension promises to employees" she started "constitute liabilities imposed on the employer. It is vital therefore to know the extent to which they are funded. If they are over provided for, there is a surplus and the company's profits have been understated. If they are underfunded, there is a deficit and the company's profits have been overstated. Since the level of a company's profitability determines its worth, it is clearly vital to investigate the funding of the scheme. If adjustments are not made to the price, either the seller is giving away an amount equal to the surplus to the buyer or the buyer incurs an additional liability equal to the deficit. Luckily we have a recent actuarial valuation for the scheme which reveals a surplus of just over £1 million."

"But that is six times the value of the company" said Sir Lancelot. "How can that be?"

"That's easy" intervened John "many pension schemes are worth more than the company nowadays. It is the result of redundancies — which produce windfall profits for the scheme — and exceptionally high investment returns over the past few years. Added to which the Magnificent Mutual's pensions actuary is very cautious in his funding assumptions."

"What this means" said Belinda "is that the company is worth much more than £150,000."

"Exactly" interrupted Frump anxious to get in on the act and seeing his bill go up by the minute. "It is worth £1,150,000. Any fool can see that" he ended, glaring at John.

"I'm afraid it is not that simple" said Belinda "because no one will pay you face value for the surplus. There are only three ways it can be used. The first is for benefit improvements for the members."

"Now why would anyone want to do that?" said Frump, the veins on his forehead standing out with amazement at the idea.

Belinda ignored this. "Secondly you can take a contribution holiday — either for the company or the members or both. Lastly the company can take a refund."

"Surely we should do that" said Sir Lancelot. "That way we will get our money out of the scheme plus the purchase price of the company."

"Well, there are a lot of technical problems to be overcome before the company can have a refund" replied Belinda. "I will just ask John to run through them." Turning to John and Belinda, Frump angrily shouted:

"You create nothing but difficulties. Give us the solutions, not the difficulties."

John quickly brought the show back on the road by saying: "Let me just list the hurdles we have to jump with an employer refund:

— It is often prohibited by the rules of the scheme. The Occupational Pensions Board are to be given power to modify scheme rules so as to allow a refund. But the power does not yet exist. Regulations will have to be made, and we don't know how the OPB will exercise its new powers.*

— It will usually require the trustees' consent and they must extract some benefit for the members in return.

— Lastly, tax at 40% has to be deducted.

The only other way the company can get its hands on the money is to take a contribution holiday. But that way it can take a long time to eliminate the surplus. It is jam spread thinly rather than in one glorious splurge."

"And so" piped up Belinda "usually the buyer and seller haggle and do a horse deal. But you only get about 50% of the face value of the surplus. It can sometimes be more if the buyer takes a contribution holiday and pays an equivalent amount to the seller by instalments as deferred consideration. Nowadays there are astute people about who will buy up a company because of its pension scheme surplus and then strip it out. Of course it helps in that situation if the seller's solicitor knows nothing about pension schemes." She blushed scarlet at this point and looked at her shoes.

Luckily Frump was so obtuse he did not take the point.

Sir Lancelot thought that matters were getting out of hand. "I suggest" he said "we adjourn for a day or two and give further thought to the problem. There is clearly more to selling a surplus than I had realised."

When Frump got back to his office, he met up with his other partner, Sidney Slicker, an obese bully in a light grey suit, grey shoes and a hectoring manner. When Frump told him of the problems with the pension scheme surplus, he promptly came up with a solution.

"Why not wind up the scheme before you sell the company. That way you avoid all the hassle with the buyer. You then provide for the current and prospective pensions. The actuary will tell you what that will cost. The balance has then got to be returned to the company. I've told you the answer in two minutes — more than that precious lot of knowalls from the Magnificent Mutual did. All they did was make you look stupid — not that that is very difficult to do."

Sid Slicker was a charmer — there was no doubt of that! He continued "You'd better get the Magnificent Mutual to give you a copy of the winding up rule and a list of members and pensioners plus the cost of buying out their benefits."

This suggestion filled Frump with hope. A couple of days later the required information came through. He and Slicker put their heads together again. Frump explained that he had looked at the winding up rule. After providing for pensions in payment, the money had to be used to provide for prospective pensions for members. After that, benefits for members had to be augmented up to Revenue limits. After that, any surplus then remaining had to be paid to the company. The actuary had provided a list of members and pensioners and calculated the cost of their benefits. There were not many people involved but he wanted to double check the list of deferred pensioners. He promised he would then calculate the Revenue limits and the cost of augmentation. The cost of providing the benefits was only £230,000.

"If we double that to provide for contingencies like augmentation, that will still leave over £500,000. So the company will get that back. We can then sell the company without all the hassle of the pension scheme. And it will be one in the eye for those clever clogs at the Magnificent Mutual who think they know more about pensions than we do", said Frump triumphantly.

"I think" replied Slicker "that you had better draft the winding up resolution and have it signed by Sir Lancelot and the trustees. The Magnificent Mutual can then wind up the pension scheme and we will get on with the sale of the company."

This was duly done. Sir Lancelot thought it was a little foolish not to wait for the actuary's figures but he was impressed with the unaccustomed speed and enthusiasm of Frump. He was anxious not to dampen that.

The winding up resolution was sent off to John Watson with instructions to wind up the scheme. This produced an immediate telephone call from John to Sir Lancelot asking him to set up an urgent meeting with Frump. He would bring the Magnificent Mutual's lawyer Archie Smithers. Frump laughed nastily when he heard about this.

"We've well and truly put the wind up the Magnificent Mutual now" he observed sarcastically and agreed to attend a meeting in Sir Lancelot's office the next day. When they all assembled John asked Sir Lancelot's permission to open the proceedings. He produced the actuary's figures which showed that the cost of providing the benefits on wind up and augmenting them up to Revenue limits would eliminate the surplus altogether. He let the awful shock sink in and then said:

"Augmenting benefits up to Revenue limits costs a lot of money and you have to include the deferred pensioners in this as well. They are included in the definition of 'member' in the rules. If it wasn't for that you'd have had your surplus all right. It's a pity you didn't take legal advice before you embarked on the winding up — or perhaps you did? At any rate I checked it out with Archie Smithers."

Frump went white as a sheet and started to bluster.

"I will not be talked down to by a load of clerks. I am the lawyer. I will interpret the rules and if they don't say what I want them to, we can amend them."

Archie thought it was time for him to intervene.

"I am afraid that it is quite clear in the rules that a deferred pensioner counts as a member. Raising your voice won't alter that. Since the scheme is being wound up, it is too late to change the rules, and in any event it must be doubtful if the trustees could agree to an amendment to the detriment of one class of members. You have really mucked things up. I have to say, Sir Lancelot, that you should obtain advice on suing your lawyers for negligence because you would have had no problem in negotiating a sale of the company which included in the price something to take account of the surplus. A competent pension lawyer should have got you about £500,000 for your surplus."

Frump could take no more and stormed out in a rage.

This unhappy tale eventually trickled out on the grapevine because Ebenezer and Frump's indemnity policy was not sufficient to cover the claim. Archie and John were talking about it at the pub one day.

"Us pensions people are in great demand nowadays" observed John a trifle smugly. Archie smilingly agreed with his old friend and said: "It is not safe to do anything without a pension lawyer on hand. But you knew that didn't you, John. We've all gone up in the world!"

Happily John had the rare ability to stand back and laugh at himself and at Archie. He brought them both back down to earth with a bump.

"But don't forget" laughed John "what goes up must come down!"


First published in *Pensions Management*, July 1989.


*Since this article was published in July 1989 the Occupational Pensions Board has been given the power to modify scheme rules to permit the refund of surpluses where:

(a) the assets of the scheme exceed liabilities by more than 5%;

(b) the trustees are satisfied that it is in the members' interests;

(c) the Inland Revenue approves; and

(d) limited price indexation — LPI — is included in the rules or in the proposals: The Occupational Pension Schemes (Modification) Regulations 1990.

# CHAPTER 12

# The Liability of Trustees

## Breach of trust

If trustees do anything that is wrong, it is called a breach of trust. If they cause loss to their members by not acting in accordance with the rules or by carelessness or fraud, they are personally liable and the trust assets can be claimed to make good the loss. Trustees thus face heavy responsibilities when they take on their duties. Not only are they responsible for their own breaches of trust, they are liable for the breaches of trust committed by their fellow trustees.

## Liabilities of trustees

Trustees can also face liability to the Inland Revenue, for example, on the 20% tax due on employee refunds or for the 40% tax charge on payments of surplus to the employer. Trustees must also comply with the rules on insider dealing. If they act on the basis of unpublished price sensitive information in marketable securities, they will commit a criminal offence.

## Corporate trustees

Sometimes trustees form a limited company to act as trustee, partly on the grounds of administrative convenience but also to limit their liability as trustees. It is doubtful, however, if there is any significant difference in the liabilities of the directors of such a company and the liabilities of individual trustees.

# Relief from the court

The position of trustees can be eased in two ways. The first is that the Trustee Act 1925 allows the court to excuse a trustee who has acted honestly and reasonably, and ought fairly to be excused. The problem here is that this remedy is dependent on the exercise of the court's discretion and so it is impossible to know in advance if a trustee will be relieved in this way. Also, the courts will not look favourably on an application for relief by a professional trustee such as a solicitor, actuary or accountant. They are expected to know better.

# Indemnity

The other way of easing the lot of trustees is to give them an indemnity. Most trust deeds indemnify a trustee against liability for breach of trust except where this is caused by wilful default. This is normally taken to mean wilful or reckless wrong doing: either knowing that the act is wrongful or not caring whether or not it is wrongful. Sometimes the employer will give an indemnity as well. This is the best protection that a trustee can obtain. A prospective trustee would be well advised to check on the terms of the indemnity before he or she accepts office.

# Principles of trusteeship

The Occupational Pensions Board in their report "Protecting Pensions" have recommended that a brief statement of the principles of trusteeship should be prepared and the disclosure requirements should be extended to include information about whether each trustee has received a copy of the statement. A statement (not yet the official version) of the principle of trusteeship appears in Chapter 23.

# CHAPTER 13

# Equal Treatment

## The background

Article 119 of the Treaty of Rome requires each Member State to ensure that men and women should receive equal pay for equal work. Pay means "the ordinary basic or minimum wage or salary and any other consideration, whether in cash or kind, which the worker receives, directly or indirectly, in respect of his employment with his employer."

If pension benefits from company pension schemes count as "pay" within Article 119, then schemes which have different pension ages for men and women will be in breach. Since 1940 the United Kingdom has had different State pension ages for men and women — 65 and 60 respectively. Occupational pension schemes have tended to follow suit and dovetail their benefits in line with the State scheme to avoid duplication.

After a number of years of uncertainty the European Court of Justice on 17.5.90 laid down in clear and unambiguous terms for the first time that pension benefits from occupational (but not State) schemes counted as pay.

## Barber v Guardian Royal Exchange

Douglas Barber was made redundant by his employer, Guardian Royal Exchange, at the age of 52. GRE paid him a lump sum redundancy payment — more than the statutory minimum. He was entitled to a pension from the GRE pension scheme from the age of 62. A woman in the same position would have received an immediate pension as well as statutory redundancy pay; the total value of her benefits would have been greater than Mr Barber's. Mr Barber claimed unlawful sex discrimination in breach of Article 119 of the Treaty of Rome.

## The judgement

The European Court of Justice ruled that:

(a) benefits paid by an employer to a worker in connection with compulsory redundancy count as "pay" within Article 119;

(b) a pension paid by a contracted-out company pension scheme counts as "pay" within Article 119;

(c) it is contrary to Article 119 for a man made compulsorily redundant to be entitled only to a deferred pension when a woman in the same position is entitled to an immediate pension as a result of an age condition that varies according to sex in the same or a similar way as the State scheme;

(d) Article 119 may be relied on directly before national courts without the need for directives from the European Comission or national legislation;

(e) Article 119 may not be relied upon to claim entitlement to a pension with effect from a date prior to that of the judgement — 17.5.90 — except where legal proceedings had already been started.

## The impact of the case

The implications of this historic decision are far reaching. Pension schemes which have been funded on the assumption that men will be entitled to pensions later than women now face a big bill to guarantee all members the same pension rights. The financial effects are so serious that the court made a rare exception from normal practice and said that its decision would not be retrospective.

The decision applies throughout the European Community but does not affect the State pension scheme or personal pension schemes. The ruling will nevertheless increase the pressure on the Government to equalise State pension ages.

## The problems

Although the judgement itself is a model of clarity, the paragraphs which rule that the decision should not be retrospective are ambiguous.

(a) The judgement could mean that the decision relates to service from 17th May onwards. This would mean that unequal benefits are permissible for service to 17th May, but for service from then unisex benefits must be provided. This is the view taken by the NAPF's counsel. It is sensible and would not lead to any back service costs.

(b) Alternatively it could mean that the decision relates to members who retire, die or leave service after 17th May. This would have the odd result that a man aged 60 who retired early on 16th May 1990 would have his pension reduced for early retirement, whereas if he retired on 17th May he would get the same unreduced pension as his female colleagues. Nevertheless it is the view which accords most closely with the actual wording of the judgement.

(c) Finally, the decision could relate to instalments of pension falling due after 17th May. This would mean that a man who took early retirement on a reduced pension before the judgement would be entitled to be paid all future instalments of his pension without reduction. This view is believed by some to be that of the European Commission.

The difference in past service costs between these views has been the subject of estimates ranging from £15 to £50 billion. Only the European Court itself can pronounce on which view is correct.

The second area of uncertainty relates to optional benefits — those that the member chooses, eg to commute part of the pension for a tax free lump sum or to take early retirement or a transfer payment to a personal pension. Commonly, optional benefits are calculated in different ways for men and women because of their different expectation of life. A woman's £1 of pension is worth more than a man's because she is likely to live about five years longer. Should benefits be of equal value or of equal amount? The European Court did not address this question. Since it was not an issue in the *Barber* case, this is hardly surprising.

In money purchase schemes does Article 119 require equal employer contributions or equal benefits or both? It seems likely that both equal employer contributions and benefits are required. But if the member exercises an option to take the cash value of the equal benefits to an insurance company, the insurance company, not being an employer bound by Article 119, can provide a conventional annuity which takes account of the member's sex and life expectancy.

In the United States the Supreme Court has decided that benefits of equal amount must be paid. Anything else is sex discrimination, whether or not it is actuarially justified. It is likely that we in Europe will move in the same direction.

But in the meantime trustees and administrators face problems which can only be solved by further test cases before the European Court. These will take time. The practical answer for trustees of schemes which have not yet equalised pension ages is to pay benefits in accordance with the rules for all service before 17.5.90 until the position is clarified. But benefits for service from 17.5.90 must be on a unisex basis.

# The options available

Because of the uncertainties many schemes may wish to take action to equalise pension ages now rather than face claims from members complaining of unequal treatment. If no action is taken, the effect of the *Barber* judgement is that, at any rate for service from 17.5.90, men have the right to retire at the same time and on the same terms as women.

The other problem is the Government's failure to equalise State pension ages. No early action is however expected, although sooner or later pressure from the European Commission will force the Government's hand.

**The options are:**

(a) *Age 60 — with reduction for early retirement*

　　　Advantages　—　　popular with trade unions
　　　　　　　　　　　　popular with some men.

　　　Disadvantages　—　very expensive
　　　　　　　　　　　　unpopular with some men and women who
　　　　　　　　　　　　　　could otherwise have worked to 65
　　　　　　　　　　　　takes away men's rights

(b) *Age 62, or any other age between 60 and 65, with reduction for early retirement*

　　　Advantages　—　　cheaper than age 60
　　　　　　　　　　　　popular with some men.

Disadvantages — expensive
unpopular with some men and women who
could otherwise have worked to 65
takes away rights from all members
likely to be wrong footed by future Government
action to equalise State pension ages.

(c) *Flexible retirement — pivotal age 65, with no reduction for retirement from age 60*

Advantages — popular with trade unions
popular with men who wish to retire early
popular with women who retain existing rights
popular with men who want to work after 60
popular with women who want to work after 60
does not affect anyone's existing rights.

Disadvantages — expensive
allows men to retire at age 60 when the
company might wish to retain them.

(d) *Age 65 — with reduction for early retirement*
Advantages — no cost — the company will save
likely to fit in with future Government action
to equalise State pension ages.

Disadvantages — takes away women's existing rights
takes away men's rights under *Barber* for
service since 17.5.90
difficult for trustees
unpopular with unions.

There are three important considerations for trustees:
  (a) The age at which employees should stop working is a matter of
employment policy for the company, not the trustees, to decide.
  (b) Unless contracts of employment are first changed, trust law will
make it difficult for trustees to agree to members' accrued benefits being reduced; this would happen if the women's pension
age is raised to 65.
  (c) There are no legal constraints on the terms to be offered to new
entrants. One option can therefore be chosen for new entrants,
another for existing members.

# Maternity and family leave

The Social Security Act 1989 contains the unfair maternity provisions which require a woman to continue to accrue pension benefits during maternity leave. The woman has to pay contributions by reference to her statutory maternity pay or her contractual pay, although for the purpose of assessing benefits, she is assumed to have received the normal pay for the job. Maternity leave covers absence due to pregnancy for which she receives either contractual or statutory maternity pay.

Unfair family leave provisions are also outlawed. This means that if a member is entitled to paid family leave, for example paternity leave, under his contract of employment, the period must be treated as pensionable. In this case benefits are assessed by reference to actual pay, not the normal pay for the job as with maternity leave.

The maternity and family leave provisions of the Act are expected to come into force on 1.1.93. The other provisions of the Act relating to the principle of equal treatment of men and women have been overtaken by the *Barber* case and are unlikely to become law. See "The Lawyer's Tale: Sex Rears its Ugly Head Again" which follows this chapter.

# The Lawyer's Tale:
# Sex Rears its Ugly Head Again

Percy Browne was the securities clerk in the Magnificent Mutual Life Assurance Society's investment department. He was an anachronism in an age of computerised administration systems, but he had worked for the company since he was 18, 43 years in all. The computer software specialists always had more pressing demands than automating Percy. When he retired, that would be different, but that was not for another four years.

Percy was a bachelor and lived with his sister. Inevitably he was set in his ways and he was teased cruelly by the young wags who worked with him. Henry, the actuary in charge, was a lax disciplinarian and did little to stop the youngsters from hassling Percy. Being an actuary, Henry was above such petty problems.

When Henry was away at an investment conference in the Bahamas, Percy went to his room to deliver some papers. He caught sight of the latest newsletter from Docs Galore, the specialist pensions documentation consultancy used by the Magnificent Mutual. His attention was drawn by the paragraph headed — "Men entitled to full pensions at age 60".

He read it going home that night. The newsletter was about a recent decision of the European Court of Justice in the case of *Barber v Guardian Royal Exchange*. Douglas Barber had been made redundant at the age of 52. Under the terms of the GRE pension scheme he was entitled to a redundancy payment and a deferred pension payable at age 62. If he had been a woman, he would have been entitled to a smaller redundancy payment but to an immediate pension. He claimed that this was unlawful sex discrimination, outlawed by the Treaty of Rome.

The GRE Pension Scheme had a normal pension age of 62 for men and 57 for women, was non-contributory and was contracted-out of the State Earnings Related Pension Scheme. The European Court decided that redundancy payments and pension benefits counted as "pay" within the terms of Article 119 of the Treaty of Rome, which requires men and women to be paid equal pay for equal work.

And so Mr Barber was entitled to retire on a full pension at age 52 because a female colleague in the same circumstances would have been entitled to do this. This rather staid narrative had an electric effect on Percy. He flew down the road from the station to his flat. His sister was astonished. "Have you just won the pools?" she asked, seeing his sparkling eyes.

"Well, in a sort of way, I have," he replied. "You know that I've had my fill of the Magnificent Mutual. I've always thought it was unjust that after 40 years of paying contributions, I still don't get a pension until I'm 65. I've thought of going early but I wouldn't get the State pension and my company pension would be reduced by 6% for each year I retire early. Because I'm not married, you won't get a dependant's pension when I die. We couldn't have afforded it."

"I know that," said Percy's sister. "So what's put the sunshine into your day?"

Percy showed his sister the newsletter. After supper they composed a letter saying that having done over 40 years with the Magnificent Mutual and reached the age of 61, he had decided to retire. He was willing to give one month's notice but would expect to go at the beginning of October. The next morning he placed the letter on Henry's desk.

He bounced into work on Monday morning. When Henry had disposed of his pile of correspondence and dismissed the last of his yuppie assistants, Percy's turn had come.

"It's a bit sudden, isn't it?" he asked Percy. "I mean you've always whinged on about not being able to afford retirement. Have you suddenly inherited some money?"

"Well, I suppose in a way I have," said Percy. He then explained to Henry about the *Barber* case and the newsletter. Henry's face darkened:

"I knew we should never have let Archie Smithers and young David go off to do their own thing on such generous terms. They spend all their time seeking publicity and charging us the earth for doing what they used to do for a fraction of the cost. You'd think they were consulting actuaries the way they carry on. I'd better get Archie to come in."

And so a meeting was arranged. Archie was accompanied by his latest assistant — a 22-year-old trainee called Rod, fashionably attired in a double-breasted check suit and black suede shoes.

Why is it, thought Henry irritably, that Archie can't do anything by himself anymore? He always has at least one assistant with him to bump up the bill.

Archie began by asking Rod to explain the background to the *Barber* decision. Rod led them through Article 118 relating to State schemes and Article 119 relating to equal pay. He told them that since 1976 Article 119 had been directly enforceable without the need for national legislation. Since the decision in 1986 in the *Bilka-Kaufhaus* case, it seemed that pension benefits counted as "pay" under Article 119. The only problem was whether a contracted-out scheme was a substitute for a State scheme — SERPS — and so governed by Article 118. If so, it could not be directly enforced. A case in 1987 — *Newstead v Department of Transport* — seemed to suggest that this was so. The matter had now been put beyond doubt by the *Barber* case.

"But the Magnificent Mutual scheme is contracted-in," said Henry, "so what's the relevance of this case? I don't like all those Euro cases. They've got nothing to do with our scheme. The rules are clear. Men can only retire early with the company's consent and there is a reduction of 6% for each year of early retirement. I'm not willing to let Percy retire. His job hasn't been programmed out; that's not until next year. He can go then with a reduction in pension as per the rules."

Percy spluttered with rage. "So you were going to get rid of me next year and throw me on the scrap heap with a hefty discount on my pension. It's my pension and I want it now. I've earned it by over 40 years' service."

"I will not be spoken to like that by a burnt-out crumbly like you," shouted Henry. "Archie, you've been unusually silent. You drafted our rules. What's gone wrong?"

"Well," said Archie, "it's all quite simple really. Perhaps Rod has unwittingly confused you by talking about old cases. Let me just try to explain. For the first time the European Court has said unambiguously that pension benefits are pay. It doesn't matter whether the scheme was contracted-in or contracted-out, contributory or non-contributory, funded or unfunded. But because the financial consequences for United Kingdom schemes would be horrendous, the Court said its decision would not be retroactive. The trouble is that no-one really knows what this means."

"Typical of lawyers," replied Henry with irritation.

"I know what it means," cried Rod. "The Court quite clearly said that the case could not be relied on in order to claim entitlement to a pension with effect from a date before that of the judgement, except where legal proceedings were already in the pipeline. You don't become entitled to a pension until you retire. Percy wants to retire now, so the reduction factor will not apply and he'll get his full pension."

"Not so fast," interrupted Archie. "The reason that the Court said its decision would not be retrospective was because that might upset the financial balance of many pension schemes. We were reasonably entitled to rely on the exception relating to pension ages in the 1986 Equal Treatment Directive and the 1989 Social Security Act and assume that occupational schemes could continue to have different pension ages. Therefore, the decision only relates to benefits which accrue after the date of the judgement — 17th May. If you look at the Court's reasoning, it is obvious that this is what they meant. And so effectively Percy will not benefit from the case except for four months' accrual of pension."

"And which of you expensive and learned gentlemen is right?" inquired Henry with icy sarcasm.

"That's easy," said Archie. "We don't know — we'll have to wait for clarification from the Courts. But there's another problem. The Magnificent Mutual scheme is contracted-in — rather unusual for an insurance company, The Court's ruling about retroactivity applies to contracted-out schemes. But it seems a reasonable inference that this part of the decision relates to *all* occupational schemes. The reasoning related, as I said, to the financial consequences and to the wording of the 1986 Equal Treatment Directive. And these reasons apply with equal force to all schemes — contracted-in or contracted-out. It seems reasonable to assume that the use of the word 'contracted-out' was a slip of the judicial pen and that the decision not to backdate the ruling applies to all schemes."

"Well," said Henry, "this is all as clear as mud. In any event Barber was about compulsory redundancy. Percy is opting for early retirement. That's different, and what's more, even if Percy has a claim for sex discrimination, that's against the company. It's nothing whatever to do with the trustees."

"Not so," replied Rod. "Trustees have to obey the law just like everyone else. The Treaty of Rome overrides all national laws and the decision takes effect immediately. Article 119 says that Member States shall ensure that men and women receive equal pay for equal work. 'Pay' is broadly defined. Pension benefits are pay. Trustees, like everyone else, have to obey the law of the land and administer their schemes in accordance with the law, not just the rules."

"And," continued Archie, "there is no logical distinction between redundancy and optional retirement. There's another case coming up next year — *Clarke v Cray Precision Engineering*.* That relates to voluntary early retirement but I don't think anyone expects the Court to reach a different conclusion. And so Percy is entitled to receive his pension at the same time and on the same terms as apply to his female colleagues."

"Any more spanners to throw in the works?" enquired Henry.

"Well a couple of little points, like you'll probably have to apply unisex commutation rates. That's enough to give any self-respecting actuary a fit of the heeby jeebies. And of course you'll have to pay Percy's sister a dependant's pension when he dies."

"Why should that be?" asked Henry. "We don't pay dependants' pensions — we pay widows' pensions. I agree that Barber would mean paying pensions to widowers where they are presently just paid to widows. But surely it only requires us to pay equal benefits regardless of sex. Since we don't pay dependants' pensions, why should we pay one to Percy's sister? It's got nothing to do with sex."

"He's got you there," said Rod to Archie. "The actuary has at least got one thing right!"

They had forgotten all about Percy sitting silently in a corner. "So my sister won't get a dependant's pension. Because most of my pension was earned before the date of the decision, it won't do me much good. All I'll get is lousy unisex commutation rates. Thanks for nothing. You two ought to be ashamed of yourselves for putting out such misleading rubbish in your newsletter. It's all for publicity, nothing for people. I'll have to stay until I'm made redundant next year after all."

First published in *Pensions Management*, September 1990.

Since this article was published in September 1990 the *Clarke* case has been settled out of court, but another similar case, *Roscoe v Hick Hargeave*, was decided in favour of the early retiree by an Industrial Tribunal.

# CHAPTER 14

# Taxation and Revenue Limits

## Taxation

### Exempt approved schemes

If an occupational pension scheme is approved by the Inland Revenue, it is then called "exempt approved". An exempt approved scheme has the following tax advantages:

(a) contributions by members are allowed for tax at their highest tax rate;

(b) contributions by employers are similarly tax deductible;

(c) employees are not taxed on the value of their employers' contributions as benefits in kind;

(d) the investment return of the scheme is exempt from income and capital gains tax;

(e) pensions are taxed as earned income;

(f) part of the member's pension can be commuted for a tax-free lump sum;

(g) lump sum death in service and death in retirement benefits can be paid free from inheritance tax.

Approved pension schemes are subject to other forms of taxation such as tax on their trading income and VAT.

## Revenue limits

Occupational pension schemes approved by the Inland Revenue are subject to various benefit limits and a limit on the amount of a member's contributions.

## Contributions

A member's contributions cannot exceed 15% of his or her taxable pay in any tax year. Taxable pay, for this purpose, is limited to £60,000 a year as from April 1989. The £60,000 cap however only affects pension schemes set up on or after 14.3.89 and new members of schemes in existence on 14.3.89 who join the scheme on or after 1.6.89. This limit will rise in line with the Retail Price Index. The current figure is £71,400 (April 1991). There is no limit as such on the amount of the employer's contributions but they must be reasonable in amount and not excessive in relation to the benefits to be provided.

## Final remuneration

The limits on benefits are defined by reference to a member's final remuneration. This is defined as either:

(a)    remuneration for any one of the five years preceding normal retirement date. Remuneration means basic pay plus fluctuating emoluments, eg bonus or commission averaged over three or more years; or

(b)    the average of total remuneration for any three or more consecutive years ending not earlier than ten years before normal retirement date.

## Dynamised final remuneration

These figures can be adjusted for inflation when final remuneration is the remuneration of a year other than the 12 months ending with the member's normal retirement date. For members who retire on or after 17.3.87 the definition of final remuneration has been changed in three ways:

(a)    by excluding gains from share options and golden handshakes;

(b)    higher paid employees earning £100,000 a year or more must use the second definition of final remuneration;

(c)    20% directors must also use the second definition of final remuneration.

A 20% director is a person who, within ten years of retirement, has been a director and either on his or her own or with associates has owned or been able to control 20% or more of the company's ordinary shares.

## Limits on pension

The normal pension limit is 1/60th of final remuneration for each year of service with a maximum of 40. Thus 40 years' service produces a pension of 40/60 of final remuneration (ie ⅔). The Revenue, however, allow a quicker build up to a pension for those members who have completed 20 years' service. In such cases a member is allowed a pension of 1/30 of final remuneration for each year of service with a maximum of 20 years (ie ⅔). But when the quicker build up of pension is taken advantage of, benefits from previous schemes or personal pensions are taken into account in the calculation. More generous calculation rules apply to members who joined their scheme before 17.3.87. Such members can get a full pension after only 10 years' service.

## Limits on lump sum benefits

Part of the member's pension may be commuted for a lump sum not exceeding ³⁄₈₀ of final remuneration for each year of service with a limit of 40. There is an increased scale for lump sums which permits commutation of 1½ times final remuneration after 20 years' service, but only if a ⅔ pension can be provided for the same period of service. There is an overall limit of £150,000 for lump sum benefits but this only applies to members who joined their scheme on or after 17.3.87. This new limit does not reduce total pension benefits. For members who joined their scheme before 17.3.87 the maximum lump sum is 1½ times final remuneration after 20 years' service.

Lastly, it is no longer possible to commute any part of the pension benefits secured by additional voluntary contribution arrangements entered into after 7.4.87.

## Limits on death benefits

A lump sum benefit on death in service of up to four times remuneration at the date of death can be paid plus a sum equal to a return of the member's contributions and interest. If the member dies within five years after retirement, a lump sum equal to the balance of five years' instalments may be paid.

## Pension benefits on death

A spouse's pension on death in service of up to ⅔ of the member's maximum approvable prospective pension is allowed. A spouse's pension on death in retirement of up to ⅔ of the member's maximum approvable pension is allowed. Similar pensions can be paid to other dependants, eg children, so long as the total of all such benefits does not exceed the member's maximum approvable pension. Children's pensions must cease on attaining the age of 18 or, if later, on ceasing full-time educational or vocational training.

## The 1989 Finance Act restrictions

The Finance Act 1989 introduced a limit on final remuneration of £60,000. Earnings in excess will be disregarded for benefit calculations. The £60,000 limit is to be index linked in line with prices. The change will affect pension schemes set up on or after 14.3.89 and new members of schemes in existence on 14.3.89 who join the scheme on or after 1.6.89. For such members therefore the maximum pension will be £40,000 a year and the maximum lump sum will be £90,000. However these figures will be increased in line with price inflation. The maximum lump sum will be ³⁄₈₀ of final remuneration for each year of service with a limit of 40, or if more, 2.25 times the amount of pension before commutation. But for the first time a full pension of ⅔ final remuneration, subject to the £60,000 limit, will be payable on or after age 50 to a member who has completed 20 years' service.

The "£60,000 limit" is now £71,400 (as at April 1991). For an illustration of the way in which Inland Revenue limits operate, see "The Lawyer's Tale: Disengaging Docs", which follows this chapter.

# The Lawyer's Tale: Disengaging Docs

The new brooms at the Magnificent Mutual Life Assurance Society were determined to make the company more profitable. Everyone had to earn their crust — even unimportant people like the docs department.

They had sent in time and motion study experts to evaluate the Magnificent Mutual's "peripheral" activities. What was a little unfortunate was that the time and motion expert had visited the docs department when Archie Smithers, in charge of the department, was on holiday, and young David, his assistant, was playing in a local cricket week and could only spare a couple of hours each morning for his work. Despite that it all got done — that was the trouble!

The experts concluded that the department should be closed and the docs work sub-contracted. Philip, the pensions actuary, accepted the recommendation. However, he was well disposed to Archie and David and by way of compromise he invited them to take part in a beauty parade to tender for the docs work.

When Archie got back from his holiday, David confronted him with the bad news:

"You and I've been made redundant, Archie. It's shocking for someone of your age. You'll never get another job. It's OK for me. I can get one with a 50% pay hike without a doubt."

Archie took the news philosophically. "I've always wanted to retire early and run a little hotel in the Cotswolds," he said. It was different, however, when he got home that evening and told his wife Bella the news.

"It's disgusting," she said. "They didn't even wait to tell you in person when you got back. They got David to do their dirty work for them. You've never been appreciated at the Magnificent Mutual. For goodness' sake, dust yourself down and go out and get a decent job."

"It's easier said than done," repeated Archie. "People don't want to know you after the age of 35. But I've got two ideas. The first is to take early retirement, sell up and buy a hotel in the Cotswolds. You and I would make a great success of that. It would be fun," he said with shining eyes.

"You can forget that for starters," said Bella. "I live for my painting, I'm not going to help you drink the profits of some crummy dump in the country. What's your second idea?"

"My second idea," said Archie, "is to set up a little business providing documentation services for insurance companies and the like. Philip said David and I could tender for the Magnificent Mutual's work. I'm sure I could get some more. I'll have to make a few phone calls."

"Well that's a bit better than your first idea," Bella replied. "But I don't want you under my feet all day, demanding cups of coffee. I've got my own life to live."

Comforted by his wife's enthusiasm Archie put his thinking cap on and took to the telephone. The following morning he went to see Philip and asked him what the Magnificent Mutual had in mind by way of severance terms.

"After all I've worked for the company for 30 years and David for seven," Archie explained.

"Well," said Philip, "we don't want to be ungenerous. We're going to put the docs work out to tender. You and David are invited to take part in a beauty parade but we are going to ask Ebenezer & Frump, the company's solicitors, and one other firm to compete. The winner will get a three year contract for all our docs work. You would of course be on the inside track, Archie."

"Thank you for nothing," bristled Archie. "After all, Ebenezer & Frump don't know anything about pensions. You're going to have to get someone to do the work. Who better than me and David?"

"Don't worry Archie," said Philip. "We'll pay a fair whack for the job and you can always take an early retirement pension. Plus you can do a little bit of other work on the side!"

The beauty parade was held. Although Archie did not realise it at the time, the result was a foregone conclusion. Naturally he was pleased to be wanted once again, but he knew he was now in a position to drive a hard bargain with Philip. And so he set out his terms.

"David and I," Archie explained, "want to set up our own company — Docs Galore — to provide documentation services for the Magnficent Mutual and anyone else who wants to use us. At my age naturally I'm worried about my pension and I don't want to be caught out by the £60,000 earnings cap."

"There is no need for you to worry about that," said Philip patronisingly. "You're not an actuary you know!"

Archie ignored this and continued, "We have decided to set up our own pension scheme, but since we're being made redundant, we expect decent severance pay plus a full past service reserve transfer value to our new scheme. We're not going to be fobbed off with cash equivalents."

"Stop fussing about details," said Philip. "It's most unlike you, Archie. I told you we'd be generous. You can both have a year's pay as compensation and of course you can have full transfer payment."

"Well," said Archie somewhat mollified. "This is what we have in mind:

— the Magnificent Mutual will establish a new subsidiary company 'Docs Galore' with a £100 share capital;

— our contracts of employment will be transferred to it;

— a new pension scheme will be set up for Docs Galore but in the interval Docs Galore will have to participate in the Magnificent Mutual scheme;

— David and I will be given an option to acquire the share capital of Docs Galore for £100 on six months' notice;

— Magnificent Mutual will enter into an agreement with Docs Galore to provide documentation services for three years."

"It's all a bit heavy, this, isn't it," said Philip in rather exasperated tones.

"Just let me finish," said Archie:

" — when we have set up the Docs Galore scheme and we've bought the shares, Docs Galore can withdraw from the Magnificent Mutual scheme;

— finally the Magnificent Mutual trustees will pay a full past service reserve transfer value, based on our pay when we leave the Magnificent Mutual scheme, to the new scheme."

"That's all, nothing very complicated; even an actuary can understand that! I'll have to get David's agreement to the details and no doubt you will want to run through all this with Ebenezer & Frump," he finished.

Ebenezer & Frump gave the plan their blessing. The truth was that they hadn't the slightest idea of what it was all about.

David, however, took a lot more persuading.

"I don't want to leave you in the lurch, Archie," he said, "but I don't know that I want all this. I must have my money at the end of each month to pay the mortgage. I'd be better off with another job. I know you're more than half way to death but I'm not. Why don't you do all this by yourself?"

"Well," said Archie, "they want us both for the docs contract. Otherwise there'd be no cover. What's more, Docs Galore is going to double our salaries."

"But Docs Galore is us," said David perplexed. "It's no good giving yourself a raise. You're just living in a fool's paradise."

"Not so," smiled Archie. "First we get a year's pay tax free. Second we get a contract for three years from the Magnificent Mutual which will guarantee our present pay index-linked. Third we can do what other work we can get. I've been making a few enquiries. We could double our work load without any trouble. That's why we can double our pay. Now do you see why I was fussing about the £60,000 limit. What's more, if it doesn't work out, I'll be the loser — you can always get another job."

"OK," said David, "I'll give it a whirl, but I must have time off for cricket and rugby. Just tell me again how it's going to work."

"Well," said Archie, "once we've set up the new company and the pension scheme, we can exercise our option to buy the shares from the Magnificent Mutual. That means that Docs Galore will no longer be a subsidiary of the Magnificent Mutual and will have to leave their pension scheme.

"At that point, we will be masters of our own destiny and can double our pay."

David still looked a bit doubtful and so Archie went on.

"What makes it seem complicated is the need to achieve three different aims:

— the first is to avoid the early leaver syndrome and get a full past service reserve transfer payment instead of cash equivalents;

— the second is to establish a new pension scheme which won't be treated by the Revenue as a new scheme and so escapes the new limits;

— the third is that if we double our pay before we leave the Magnificent Mutual scheme, we will double the transfer payment."

"OK — details, details," said David, beginning to tire of the conversation. "I can see that if we get a past service reserve, we do a lot better than cash equivalents. I like the idea of doubling our pay. I also twig that if we do that at the right time, we'll double our transfer payment. Won't old Philip be hopping mad when he finds out? I'd love to be a fly on the wall when someone tells him the good news."

"That only leaves the other aim," said Archie, "of making sure that our scheme won't be treated as a new scheme. I have looked into this and checked out the Transitional Provisions Regulations. The Revenue won't apply the new restrictions in the Finance Act 1989 or the Finance (No 2) Act 1987, come to that, when benefits under the old basis cease to accrue under a scheme for a member who joins another scheme established by an associated employer. What is vital is that when the Docs Galore scheme is set up, Docs Galore Ltd is owned by the Magnificent Mutual so as to fall within the terms of the regulations. It won't then count as a new scheme and the subsequent change of ownership of the shares won't alter the position. We then exercise our option to buy the shares, acquire the business and give ourselves a pay rise."

"But I'm not earning £60,000 a year," said David.

"Not yet, you're not," continued Archie. "But I will be after we've doubled our pay. In any case we were both members of the Magnificent Mutual scheme before 17th March 1987. I don't want any cap on my tax free lump sum. It would be crazy to throw away advantages like that."

"OK I agree," said David. "It seems a pretty smart scheme you've dreamed up Archie. Not bad for someone more than half their way to death."

"That's better than being half dead, which is what you often seem like on a Monday morning, David," replied Archie cheerfully.

"What about moving on to a more exciting topic like company cars. We'll both be directors of Docs Galore. We'll obviously have to do a lot of travelling. What kind of car takes your fancy?"

"That's easy," replied David, quick as a flash, his interest immediately aroused. "I'll have a nice new shiny red Porsche."

First published in *Pensions Management*, March 1990.

# CHAPTER 15

# *Surpluses*

## What is a surplus?

A surplus is simply an excess of the resources of the scheme over its liabilities. The Finance Act 1986 introduced a statutory test for calculating the amount of past service surplus under which it has to be calculated by reference to a set of assumptions laid down by the Government actuary. The assumptions relate both to the value of the assets as well as the benefits. This is known as "the prescribed basis".

## The rules for eliminating surpluses

The Finance Act 1986 lays down that unless a scheme is to lose a proportionate part of its tax exemptions, then a surplus, calculated on the prescribed basis, has to be eliminated within a five year period. For this purpose a surplus exists if the assets of the scheme exceed its liabilities by more than 105%. The permitted ways of achieving this are:
   (a)   a refund to the employer,
   (b)   benefit improvements,
   (c)   a contribution holiday for the members,
   (d)   a contribution holiday for the employer, or
   (e)   any combination of these methods.

## The tax charge

A refund to the employer or a combination of methods which includes a refund must not result in the assets being reduced to less than 105% of the scheme's liabilities. A free standing tax charge of 40% is levied on a refund and has to be deducted at source by the trustees. There are no offsetting tax allowances. No payment to an employer can be made without the written consent of the Inland Revenue.

# Refunds of surplus to the employer

Some scheme rules prevent a refund of surplus being paid to an employer. If the trustees' consent to a rule change is required, to enable such a payment to be made, they will have to secure some benefit improvement for their members in return for giving their consent. Permitting an employer's refund would not normally be considered to be in the interests of the members. The trustees must come to some agreement with the employer about the division of the surplus between a refund on the one hand and benefit improvements on the other.

# Modification orders

Some trust deeds may prevent both a refund and a rule change to permit it. Where this is the case the Occupational Pensions Board has been given power to modify the rules where:

(a) an actuary's certificate, as calculated for Inland Revenue purposes, shows that the scheme's assets exceed liabilities by more than 5%;

(b) the trustees are satisfied that it is in the members' interests that the surplus is eliminated in the way proposed;

(c) the proposals have been approved by the Inland Revenue;

(d) the scheme provides for guaranteed pension increases — limited pension indexation or LPI — or a provision for LPI is included in the proposals.

Where there is no indication that benefit improvements or contribution holidays are part of the package, the Occupational Pensions Board may require further information.

For an illustration of the kind of problems that can arise, see "The Lawyer's Tale: Sticky Fingers" which follows this chapter.

# The Lawyer's Tale:
# Sticky Fingers

Major Grabit was the sole equity partner in Sue, Grabit and Run, a medium sized firm of City solicitors. He was a churchwarden and a man of undoubted probity, if not of intellect. He was also a humbug of the first order. Under his reign, Sue Grabit and Run had gone downhill as relentlessly as other City firms had climbed up.

Sue, Grabit and Run had a staff pension scheme administered by the Magnificent Mutual Life Assurance Society. The time for the scheme's triennial actuarial valuation had arrived and the actuary's report giving details of a surplus of £500,000 had arrived on Major Grabit's desk.

The Magnificent Mutual's actuary had said that the surplus had now reached a point where the Revenue would require action to reduce it by:

— improving benefits;

— having a contribution holiday for the firm or the members or both; or

— paying a refund to the employers.

The actuary explained in tedious detail how the surplus had been calculated under the new regulations and the various options available for reducing it to the statutory minimum of 5% of the excess of assets over liabilities. If they did not, they would lose the valuable tax reliefs attributable to the excess part of the fund. All this was quite beyond the wit of the Major. He had no idea what to do. So he summoned John Watson, the pensions superintendent at the Magnificent Mutual who was responsible for the Sue, Grabit and Run Staff Benefits Scheme. John arranged to meet Major Grabit the following week.

He took along, to give him experience, a smart young man on his team called Martin, who wore a fashionable light grey suit, lemon yellow tie and black suede shoes.

John Watson and his assistant Martin were ushered in to meet the Major, and explained the various options to the trustees. The staff scheme was a good contracted-out scheme that had been in existence for many years. It was a legacy from the days when Sue, Grabit and Run had been a respected name in legal circles. There were only 15 members and in fact there was not that much scope for increasing benefits.

The pensions being paid to existing pensioners could be improved significantly because little had been done about this in the past. When inflation had been high in the 70s, Major Grabit reckoned the scheme could not afford any pension increases. Now that inflation was low, he reckoned that the pensioners did not need a rise. It would only make them improvident, he added hypocritically.

John Watson had worked out a benefit improvement package that would compensate the pensioners for the ravages of past inflation and that would provide for automatic 5% escalation in the future. That and some other minor improvements had been costed at about £150,000; he suggested that the other £350,000 be eliminated by a contribution holiday both in relation to the firm's 10% contribution and the staff's 5% contributions. He reckoned that this would take care of the surplus in three to four years.

"You could, of course, take a refund for the firm, if you wished, but there are some technical difficulties about this, which do not apply to my recommended course of action".

There was a lengthy pause during which you could almost hear the Major's brain cogs whirring away. Eventually he said:

"But how did we ever get a surplus like this? I thought we just paid contributions to provide the staff with their pensions."

John explained that there were various methods of funding pension schemes. When the scheme was set up, the actuary recommended the "aggregate funding" method. This meant that contributions were calculated having regard to the members of the scheme, their potential service and estimated salary increases. This took no account of new, younger members joining and so was a fairly conservative method of funding. There were, of course, other funding methods such as the "projected accrued benefit" method. This had been adopted by the Government Actuary as the method for calculating the surplus under the terms of the Finance Act 1986. It takes account of accrued service to the date of valuation and projected salary increases to retirement attributable both to inflation and promotion. There was also the discontinuance method . . . "For goodness sake, stop", cried Major Grabit, "my head is reeling — what on earth does it all mean?"

John's assistant, Martin, seeing his chance, jumped into the discussion.

"Pay no attention to the mumbo jumbo, Major. It's all quite simple really. It all depends on how much you pay into the piggy bank each month. If you pay in too much, you end up with a surplus; if you pay in too little, you end up with a deficit. Actuaries look at the membership data, look back on what has happened in the past and then predict the future. If you drive a car looking out of the back window, you'd get it wrong too. Of course, they dress it up with fancy names, like John said. But it's still mumbo jumbo, when all is said and done."

John was horrified. "It's not quite like that, Major Grabit. But the lad has a gift for simple explanation," he said with a barbed look at his assistant. He rushed on "Then, of course, there is the great increase in the value of the fund's investments over the last few years. So really your surplus is the product of rather too conservative funding assumptions and the effect of the bull market in the 1980s."

"But" the Major continued, "did I understand that, as employers, one of our options is to take out the entire £500,000 from the fund?"

The prospect was evidently a mouthwatering one, as the Major was the sole partner now left in the firm.

"Yes, of course," said John. "It is all set out in the actuary's report" he continued patiently, "but would attract a tax charge of 40%, even if you had tax losses or allowances that would otherwise be available to set against the charge. In other words the charge to tax is what the Revenue call 'free-standing', although it would not apply to charities."

"But I pay tax at 60%", said the Major, "and in any event I could postpone the day of reckoning for some time".

"Not so" interrupted John quickly "the trustees have to deduct the tax from the refund and pay it over to the Revenue."

"Well, anyway," rejoined Major Grabit "60% of a loaf is better than no bread. It amounts to —" there was an awkward pause as he looked at his fingers, "£350,000."

John was tempted to offer him a pocket calculator. At any rate he would at least then make his mistakes more quickly. He restrained himself, however, and gently pointed out that the correct figure was only £300,000.

"I had not realised the significance of this possibility" Major Grabit said with practised disingenuousness. "Quite clearly we must take the refund. It would only confuse the staff if we talked about improving their benefits. They would only think they were no good now. As for the pensioners, they must learn to draw in their belts. It would not do to encourage extravagance. We as employers are the trustees of the scheme and in the interests of our beneficiaries, we must take the extra amount as a refund forthwith."

John quite clearly had not foreseen this and was rather aghast. He turned to Martin, who, seeing the worry in his boss's face, quickly piped up and said:

"But you can't do this if you are both employer and trustee and in any event the scheme rules forbid it."

"How dare you talk to a learned man of the law in those terms, you impertinent young whippersnapper" shouted Major Grabit angrily.

John Watson waded in to calm the crisis and suggested that as there were certain legal problems, a meeting should be arranged with Smithers, the Magnificent Mutual's lawyer. "Pensions are getting terribly complicated nowadays — what with all the new laws that Parliament keeps churning out and Smithers is a member of the Association of Pension Lawyers. I think you have to be one of those to advise on a pensions matter" he finished blandly.

So Smithers was dusted down and led out to Sue, Grabit and Run the following day. He briefly explained the legal problems.

"You cannot, as employers and trustees, take the entire surplus as an employer's refund. That must be a breach of trust and a disgruntled member could sue you."

"We've got plenty of them" said the Major "but they need never know."

"I'm afraid they will" Smithers said. "The Occupational Pensions Board will insist on them being consulted. In addition there are new disclosure regulations which require the preparation of an annual trustees' report and audited accounts. These have to be made available to members and their availability publicised."

"We might as well live in Russia and have done with it" said Major Grabit in a choleric rage. "I am the best judge of what is good for the staff."

"At any rate" resumed Smithers quickly "I am afraid you will either have to appoint independent trustees or arrange for the members to be separately advised. There is a clear conflict of interest here and anything less could involve you in an action for breach of trust.

"You will also have to change the scheme rules. At the moment they preclude a refund to the employer and they will have to be altered to allow this. Under the power of alteration in your rules this is prohibited.

You will therefore have to apply to the Occupational Pensions Board for a dispensation to enable you to do this. The OPB can, and no doubt will, impose conditions. As I indicated, one of these will presumably be a requirement to consult the members, and obtain their views. We will not be able to do this yet because the regulations permitting this are not in force."*

"Have you finished throwing spanners in the works?" demanded the Major angrily. "I cannot think how the Magnificent Mutual could employ an obvious Bolshevik like you!"

"I'm afraid there is still one more hurdle" rejoined Smithers silkily. "You require the trustees' consent to effect the rule change. As I have indicated, there should be independent trustees. At the risk of an immediate deportation order to Russia, may I suggest that they will inevitably require some give and take as a condition of their consent. And finally, the Revenue must give its consent before a refund is paid to the employer."

At this point the veins on old Grabit's forehead began to swell ominously. Smithers, sensing danger, quickly finished:

"May I ask you to reconsider John Watson's recommendation? He is, after all, one of our best pensions superintendents. He has your interests at heart, but you really cannot treat your pension scheme like a money box. It is a trust fund — with all that that implies. I suggest that you reflect on John Watson's proposals, and talk to your staff. It might then be appropriate to have another meeting with John Watson."

"Are all solicitors like that?" John asked Smithers later in the day.

"No, of course not. There are good and bad solicitors just as there are good and bad pensions superintendents. But seriously, would it not have been better if the Government had grasped the nettle and required surpluses to be used to augment benefits up to Revenue limits or for contribution holidays, and only to have allowed employer refunds as a last resort when there was no other way of getting rid of the surplus. That would have had the merit of flexibility and kept the sticky fingers out of the money box."

First published in *Pensions Management*, January 1987.

*Since the article was published in January 1987, the Occupational Pensions Board has been given the power to modify scheme rules to permit a refund of surplus. Furthermore the Social Security Act 1990 precludes any payment to the employer out of the scheme until LPI — limited price indexation — has been guaranteed for all pensions in payment. The story in the article shows the value of this reform.

# CHAPTER 16

# An Outline of State Pensions, Occupational Pensions and Personal Pensions

## State pensions

### The old age pension — flat rate

The State pension scheme consists of two parts — the basic flat rate State retirement pension and the earnings related supplement — the State Earnings Related Pension Scheme (SERPS). The basic flat rate State retirement pension (the old age pension) is (as at April 1991) £52.00 per week for a single person and £83.25 per week for a married couple. It is dependent on having made enough National Insurance contributions and is, so far at any rate, not means tested. It is payable at age 65 for a man and age 60 for a woman, although the EC has published a draft directive requiring equalisation of State pension ages.

### The State Earnings Related Pension Scheme

Unless an employee becomes a member of an occupational pension scheme which is contracted out of SERPS, he or she will pay full rate National Insurance contributions and receive an additional earnings related pension based on earnings between the lower earnings limit (as at April 1991) — £52.00 per week and the upper earnings limit (as at April 1991) — £390.00 per week. The SERPS pension is based on a percentage of revalued average lifetime earnings. The SERPS pension is also payable at age 65 for men and 60 for women. Earnings above the upper earnings limit are not pensionable under SERPS.

### State pensions not funded

Both the flat rate and the earnings related pension, when they come to be paid, are revalued in line with prices. They operate on a pay as you go system — that is, out of current Government revenue. They are not funded out of contributions invested separately and set aside.

### Contracting out

It is possible to contract out of SERPS by joining a scheme which promises equivalent benefits or by paying minimum contributions to an employer's scheme or a personal pension. A scheme which is contracted out of SERPS by paying equivalent benefits is very different from a scheme which is contracted out on the basis of paying minimum contributions. This aspect is considered under the next heading.

# Occupational pensions

### Money purchase schemes

Occupational pension schemes are sponsored by an employer who has to contribute to the scheme. They are either defined contribution (or money purchase) schemes or defined benefit (or salary related) schemes. Money purchases schemes are simple and produce for each member a pot of money when he or she retires which is the product of the employee's and employer's contributions plus their investment return. This pot of money is then used partly to provide a tax-free lump sum for the member and, as to the rest, a pension for the member, spouse and dependants, as he or she chooses.

### Salary related schemes

A salary related scheme does not depend on the amount of the contributions or the investment return. It guarantees the members a pension related to their salaries when they retire. Members do not, therefore, have to worry about inflation during their working lives or about stock market conditions. A salary related scheme which is contracted out of SERPS has to guarantee benefits equivalent to the SERPS benefits foregone, thus providing guaranteed minimum pensions. This means what it says — they are ultimately guaranteed by the State.

## Money purchase contracting out

A money purchase scheme which is contracted out of SERPS does not have to provide equivalent or guaranteed benefits. Here contracting out of SERPS is on the basis of minimum contributions — the difference between full rate National Insurance contributions and reduced rate National Insurance contributions on earnings between the lower and upper earnings limits. Because the member is contracted out of SERPS, the member and the employer do not have to pay for SERPS benefits, hence the difference between the two rates of National Insurance contributions. The only requirement here is that the minimum contributions must be invested on a money purchase basis to provide a pension for the member and his or her spouse. What that pension will be cannot be known in advance and depends on the amount of the contributions and the investment return, and annuity rates when the member retires. It is not guaranteed.

## Personal pensions

Personal pensions are simply a method of providing for old age on an individual, rather than a collective, basis. They are attractive to a Government which dislikes collectivism. They were invented in 1956 for the self employed and those who had no pension scheme open to them. In 1988 they were extended in two ways. Employers were for the first time allowed to contribute and it became possible to contract out of SERPS on the basis of minimum contributions through a personal pension. They are money purchase schemes.

For an illustration of the differences between an employer-sponsored pension scheme and a personal pension, see "The Lawyer's Tale: Sowing the Seeds for a Good Company Scheme", which follows this chapter.

# The Lawyer's Tale:
# Sowing the Seeds for a Good
# Company Scheme

Robin Hathersage was the 50-year-old proprietor of Hathersages Garden Centres, a chain which flourished in the affluent home counties. He started his first garden centre just outside Sevenoaks in the 1950s and with a combination of good marketing and skilful display of plants, trade boomed. He took in his sister to help run the administrative side of the business.

In the last seven years they had opened a new branch every year and had hit on the brainwave of setting up garden conservatories — glass shops by any other name — in the inner city areas. The first was in Kensington and a second in Docklands soon followed. The conservatories were lavishly stocked with the most beautiful and, naturally, expensive plants and garden accessories. They went a bomb with the yuppies — on a Saturday morning you could hardly move for Hooray Henries.

Soon after Hathersages got going, they set up a pension scheme for the permanent staff with the Magnificent Mutual Life Assurance Society. The superintendent in charge of the scheme was one of the best, John Watson. He ran his schemes and his team of six assistants like a sheepdog with a flock of sheep. John had a great following among his clients and pensions administrators competed to get on his team.

Robin Hathersage and his sister, Melissa, were both now of the age to be interested in pensions and their interest was stimulated by the continuous stream of articles that appeared in the quality papers each weekend: Comps, FSAVCs, APPs — the acronyms poured out like a flood. Robin and Melissa soon realised that the world was about to change and that they would have to do something about their pension scheme.

They had read that membership would be voluntary from 6 April

1988 and that employees would be free to take out personal pensions. But although they were both intelligent, well read people, they did not understand how it would affect them.

They turned to John Watson, who said that he was running a series of roadshows and would put Hathersages next on the list. The following week, John and his young assistant Belinda appeared at the head office in Sevenoaks. John explained that they would give a pensions presentation to the staff: but before they could do this, they needed to know the company's thinking on pensions.

John's technique was to let Belinda make the running and do the main work of the meeting, leaving him free to field any difficult questions. Belinda explained that most employers set up pension schemes so that their employees were not left destitute in their old age. There was a "me too" element as well. Companies, like humans, don't want to be left behind and they therefore imitate the leaders. She went on to point out that companies have, until now, been able to make membership compulsory so that employees are locked in willy nilly. "Nothing wrong with that," interrupted John. "It means that schemes can cover the whole workforce and achieve economies of scale in areas such as life cover and administration. But from 6 April you can no longer make an employee join a scheme nor can you prevent an existing member from leaving. If an employee opts out, he can either take out a personal pension or join the State Earnings Related Pension scheme."

"I still don't know what we have got to do," said Robin Hathersage. "Can you please explain to my sister and me in simple terms just what the Government changes mean."

"Right," said Belinda. "First the changes:
— Serps benefits are to be cut back so that anyone retiring after the year 2000 will get a much lower State Earnings Related Pension;
— scheme membership is to become voluntary;
— schemes which are contracted out of SERPS — like yours — will have to provide pensions for widowers as well as widows;
— contracted-out schemes will be inflation proofed with guaranteed minimum pensions in payment having a ceiling of 3%. This has, up to now, been the responsibility of the DSS;
— schemes will have to provide voluntary contribution facilities;
— schemes will be able to contract out of SERPS on the basis of a minimum contribution — used to buy money purchase benefits to provide protected rights;

— members will be able to take out personal pensions and contract out of SERPS on the minimum contribution basis;

— members have the right to make free standing AVCs — they can choose their own investment medium for voluntary contributions — they are no longer forced to use the scheme's own facility."

At this point, Melissa Hathersage was nodding off and her brother's face was covered with confusion.

"Don't worry, Mr Hathersage," said John, "Belinda has just induced an attack of that well known disease — mego — otherwise known as 'my eyes glaze over'. It is a common enough affliction brought on by listening to pensions consultants."

"It is very simple really," he went on to explain. "You have two questions to answer. First, do you care whether people join your scheme or not? Clearly, if you don't mind whether they join, there is no point in trying to make the scheme more attractive to discourage people from taking out personal pensions."

"No," said Robin Hathersage, "from what I have read, for most employees personal pensions will not be as good as a final salary contracted-out scheme like ours. A personal pension is OK for high fliers but there aren't many of these in the garden trade and we don't have a high staff turnover. So Melissa and I would want to encourage people to join. How can we achieve that?"

"Well," said John, "in two ways. A scheme like yours gives valuable family protection if an employee dies in service — life cover of twice salary plus spouse's and children's pensions. You don't get that as of right with a personal pension. So the first question you have to decide is whether you will continue to give this benefit to members who opt out. If you refuse, you will make personal pensions much less attractive. The additional protection will have to be bought separately and expensively by the employee. On the other hand, you will have to consider how you will be able to face the widow of an employee who had opted out for a personal pension. It is a very difficult decision."

"I can see that," said Robin Hathersage. "Is there no half way house? Instead of giving someone who opts out the full family protection, could we just give a lump sum benefit?"

"Yes, you can," said Belinda. "You can give any combination of benefits, or indeed none at all in this situation."

"You said there was a positive way of promoting the scheme," said Robin Hathersage.

"Yes, there is," replied Belinda. "You must make a virtue out of necessity and sell the scheme to your employees. I know there are some employers who will take the opportunity to close down their schemes or just let them linger on for those who want to join. After all, they will save money if employees opt for personal pensions.

"But if you want to freshen up the scheme, you could reduce the entry age from 25 to 18. In that way, the personal pension salesmen won't have it all their own way for those vital years. You could maybe reduce the members' contributions so that they won't save any money by not joining. If you did these two things, with the life cover protection you offer and a good communications exercise, you should give the personal pension touts a run for their money."

"The trouble with final salary schemes like yours," said John, "is that people who leave before retirement have had a raw deal. That's what makes personal pensions attractive. They move with you. But you can get the best of both worlds by having what is called a money purchase underpin."

"My goodness me," interrupted Melissa, "you pensions people do talk a lot of gobbledeygook. You make my poor head spin."

"A money purchase underpin is very simple really," continued John. "It only means that people who leave get the value of both their own and the company contributions plus a reasonable rate of return. Another, but more complicated way, is to have two schemes — a money purchase scheme for everyone, but with the right to join a final salary scheme at, say age 40 to 45. That gives you the best of both worlds but it is of course more difficult to administer. One other thing that Belinda forgot to mention," he said, "is that an employee who opts out of the company scheme has no right to join at a later date. You can permit this if you want. My suggestion is to allow it at the company's discretion. That way you have complete flexibility."

"Well," said Mr Hathersage, "luncheon beckons. You two have done us proud. I now understand everything completely. I shall explain it to all my friends at the golf club on Sunday and see them get an attack of mego!"

First published in *Pensions Management*, April 1988.

# CHAPTER 17

# Contracting Out

An employee can be contracted out of the State Earnings Related Pension Scheme (SERPS) either at his employer's election or of his own choice. If an employee joins an occupational pension scheme, the decision to contract out is that of the employer, although the employees and recognised trade unions must be consulted first. An employee can make his or her own decision to contract out by taking out an appropriate personal pension.

Contracting out must either be on the basis of guaranteed minimum pensions or minimum contributions.

## Guaranteed minimum pensions

In this case the National Insurance contributions of both employer and employee are reduced. The amount of the pension payable from the scheme must not be less than the guaranteed minimum pension. This is roughly equivalent to the pension that the member would have earned from SERPS if he or she had not been contracted out. Any shortfall between the amount of the guaranteed minimum pension and the notional SERPS entitlement is paid by the Department of Social Security to the member at State pension age.

## Revaluation of guaranteed minimum pensions

Guaranteed minimum pensions are revalued until State pension age in line with national average earnings. If the member leaves the scheme, the scheme has to revalue the guaranteed minimum pension up to State pension age. There are three ways in which schemes may do this:

(a) at a fixed rate of 7.5% a year, or

(b) in line with national average earnings, or

(c) at a lower fixed rate of 5% a year.

If 5% revaluation is adopted, the scheme has to pay a premium to the Department of Social Security to cover the risk of additional revaluation. From the member's point of view, whichever method of revaluation is adopted is immaterial, because any shortfall will be made up by the Department of Social Security at State pension age.

## Minimum contributions

It is now possible to contract out of SERPS on the basis of minimum contributions by the employer and the employee. Minimum contributions consist of the contracted-out rebate — the difference between full rate and reduced rate National Insurance contributions on earnings between the lower and upper earnings limits (see the previous chapter for an explanation of these terms). This method of contracting out can be through an employer's scheme (a contracted-out money purchase scheme) or on a personal basis through an appropriate personal pension.

## Protected rights

Contracting out on the basis of minimum contributions produces protected rights instead of guaranteed minimum pensions. The SERPS pension is reduced in just the same way as if the member had been in a contracted-out final salary scheme. But because he or she is in a money purchase scheme, and not a final salary scheme, the member gets money purchase benefits. Protected rights are therefore money purchase benefits and they represent what can be bought with the proceeds of the minimum contributions. This may be less or more than guaranteed minimum pensions. It is important to recognise that guaranteed minimum pensions are defined benefits revalued in line with the national average earnings until State pension age; and they are guaranteed. Protected rights, like all money purchase benefits, are not defined; nor are they guaranteed.

Pensions payable from SERPS are revalued in line with prices (not earnings) by the Department of Social Security when they come to be paid. Guaranteed minimum pensions earned up to 5.4.88 are not revalued by the occupational scheme but the Department of Social Security meets the cost of price indexation. Guaranteed minimum pensions earned from 6.4.88 and protected rights pensions have to be increased in payment in line with prices, with a ceiling of 3% a year, by the occupational or personal pension scheme. The Department of Social Security meets the balance of the cost of indexation. Accordingly once the guaranteed minimum pension or protected rights pension comes into payment, then from the member's or the member's spouse's viewpoint, the pension is revalued in line with prices either by the scheme or by the Department of Social Security, or from both sources.

# CHAPTER 18

# Preservation

## Preserved benefits

### Refund of contributions

A member who leaves a pension scheme with less than two years' qualifying service is usually only entitled to a refund of his or her own contributions; and even this right does not arise unless conferred by scheme rules. Tax at 20% is deducted by the trustees together with the member's share of the contributions equivalent premium. This premium is payable if the scheme is contracted out and represents the cost of buying the member back into SERPS.

### Preserved pension

After two years' qualifying service a member must receive a preserved pension. A member must also receive a preserved pension if the scheme accepted a transfer value from a personal pension previously taken out by the member. This preserved pension is based on pay and service at the date of leaving and is payable at the scheme's normal retirement date. In a money purchase scheme the member's preserved pension is based on the amount standing to his or her credit in the scheme at the date of leaving.

### Qualifying service

Qualifying service is pensionable service under the rules of the scheme plus the actual period of service in a previous scheme from which a transfer payment has been made to the present scheme. Qualifying service also includes waiting periods. These are periods during which a member waits to join the scheme which then is counted as pensionable. Qualifying service is not interrupted by breaks of one month or less or by maternity absence, or absences in furtherance of a trade dispute.

## Leaving the pension scheme but not the job

Since 6.4.88 members have the right to leave a pension scheme even if they do not leave their job.

## Revaluation

If a member left a scheme before 1.1.86 there is no requirement to revalue his or her preserved pension. If the member left the scheme on or after 1.1.86 but before 1.1.91 part of the preserved pension is revalued in line with prices with a ceiling of 5%. The part of the pension that is revalued in this way is the part earned by service from 1.1.85; service before that date does not have to be revalued. If, however, the member left on or after 1.1.91 the whole of the preserved pension has to be revalued in line with prices up to the 5% limit. There is no revaluation if the member leaves within one year of the scheme's normal retirement date. In a contracted-out scheme it is only the pension in excess of the guaranteed minimum pension that is revalued in this way. The method of revaluing the guaranteed minimum pension is explained in Chapter 17.

In the case of a money purchase scheme the amount standing to the member's credit in the scheme is revalued by adding to it the investment yield, for example interest or bonuses.

# CHAPTER 19

# Transfers

### The right to a transfer

A member who leaves a scheme on or after 1.1.86 with a preserved pension can transfer the cash equivalent of the pension to a new employer's scheme or to a personal pension or to a buy-out policy.

### Conditions for exercising the option

The member must exercise this option in writing but can withdraw it at any time until the trustees have done all that is required of them to enter into the transfer arrangement. The member must exercise the option by the later of six months after leaving or one year before his normal retirement date. The trustees have 12 months from the member's formal application to pay the transfer value. But if it is not paid within six months, then the payment has to be recalculated and the recalculated value paid or interest added to the original amount, if this would produce a larger amount.

### Calculation of transfer value

The transfer value is the cash equivalent of the member's accrued benefits. It must be calculated using methods and assumptions approved by an actuary and in accordance with the professional guidelines published by the Institute and Faculty of Actuaries. It must also be calculated in a way which is consistent with the methods and assumptions used to calculate benefits to be given in return for transfer payments from another scheme. Where it is the established custom of the trustees to award discretionary pension increases, the cash equivalent has to be increased to take this into account, unless the trustees make a direction to the contrary. The amount of a transfer value may also be subject to reduction if the scheme is in deficit.

If a member leaves the scheme but not his or her job, the right to a cash equivalent is restricted to the proportion of his or her accrued rights which has arisen since 6.4.88 unless the scheme rules permit the whole of the accrued rights to be transferred.

## New employer's scheme

A new employer's scheme, in order to be able to accept a transfer, must either be a statutory scheme, or one which is fully approved by the Inland Revenue. If the scheme is not yet fully approved because, for example, it is still operating on the basis of an Interim Trust Deed, the Revenue's consent to the transfer must be obtained.

## Buy-out policies

If the member wishes to transfer to a buy-out policy, then the policy must satisfy the requirements of the Inland Revenue and the insurance company must be authorised by the Department of Trade and Industry. The member can have as many policies as he or she wants.

## Personal pensions

Members can also transfer their cash equivalent to a personal pension. The member must consent in writing and the transfer value must be used to buy money purchase benefits.

For an illustration of some of the problems that can arise on transfers, readers are referred to "The Lawyer's Tale: Shutting the Stable Door", which follows this chapter.

# The Lawyer's Tale: Shutting the Stable Door

Archie Smithers sat on the edge of the turquoise waters of Horseshoe Bay, Bermuda sifting the soft, pink, sugarlike sand through his fingers. He had had to go to Bermuda at short notice to attend a couple of board meetings and make a presentation. He was more than a little irritated that his colleagues at Docs Galore, young David and Matt in particular, were grumbling about his champagne life style. As he said to his wife Bella, who had insisted on coming with him, "Life is not a bed of roses. We've had a long transatlantic flight and had to meet a whole lot of new people. Matt and David sometimes have no idea of all the things I have to do!"

Just before he came away, his actuary friend Colin Bell had asked him to give independent advice to the trustees of a pension scheme about a bulk transfer. The company was a large brewery company which had divested itself of its cider manufacturing business. It was a management buy out and the company had wished to see the new business off to a good start.

The pension scheme had a huge surplus and the company had enjoyed a contribution holiday for many years. Since the surplus arose largely from the massive redundancies of a few years back, plus good investment returns, the company thought it should pay a transfer value based on a share of the fund. It was quite happy to let the buyers continue to enjoy the contribution holiday. But since there were doubts about the viability of the business, it built in some protective conditions for the transferring members — for a period of three years from the sale:

- if the new scheme was wound up, the entire fund would be used for the members;
- there could be no self-investment or loans to the company;
- any member leaving because of dismissal or redundancy would get his or her share of the fund.

Somewhat unusually, a supplementary agreement was entered into by which the trustees of the buyer's scheme gave an undertaking to the transferring scheme trustees to apply the conditions when administering the new scheme.

Colin relayed this to Archie before he went away and said he would send him the papers. The management buy out was heading for the rocks. It was mortgaged up to the hilt at the bank and needed a quick fix from the pension scheme.

As Colin explained:

"It's not an easy situation, Archie. The new company has invested heavily in new equipment; it's about to embark on a redundancy programme. They are two years down the line and they need a further year to turn the tide. Everyone seems to think they will do it but the bank won't play ball and advance any more money. Just to put the figures in focus, the sale price was £3 million and the transfer payment includes £7 million worth of surplus. It's all a bit embarrassing really. We had no idea the figure would be so large but when we did our sums, that's what it turned out to be."

"And so," said Archie, "what the sellers actually did was give away the business plus £4 million."

"Don't wade in with your hob nailed boots," said Colin. "We didn't give away £4 million. We locked it in for the benefit of the members. That's the rub. The new company has said it would like a loan now. If it gets it, it can then start what it calls the 'necessary remedial therapy'!"

"In other words," said Archie, "sacking the members."

"Well, yes and no," replied Colin. "But there will be less sacked if it's done now than if it is left until later. We're in a cleft stick. If we lend the company the money now and it goes down the tube, the members who were made redundant won't be very pleased. If we refuse and the company goes belly up, the members will lose their jobs. And if the company limps on for another year, it can wind up the pension scheme and pocket the entire surplus because the protective conditions will have expired then.

"We have been asked to release the protective conditions 12 months early. It's all very delicate because the finance director is mad with us for underestimating the surplus so badly at the time of the sale. We need your help, Archie."

"Send me the papers," said Archie "and I'll get the boys to run through them and fax them to me."

As Archie was not over-endowed with business in Bermuda, he had plenty of time to study the faxes that came in each evening from London. Archie looked at the day's faxes while enjoying a rum swizzle. He made a few notes and the following morning he spoke to the boys in London. As Matt said sarcastically to David:

"This way we get better value from Archie than when he's at his desk. He's always on the phone or dashing off to meetings and doesn't always have as much time for my problems as I want. Whereas now, when his meetings are over, his only distraction is Bella. They've been married for so long they don't communicate with each other any more, so he can spend the evening thinking about our problems."

"Well," laughed David, "there are other things in life apart from talking to your wife and thinking about faxes."

"No," said Matt, "if I didn't keep him occupied, he'd only be drinking cocktails or enjoying himself. You know how I disapprove of that!"

The following week Archie was back in London in a meeting with the trustees. Could they enforce the protective conditions if the new trustees chose to ignore them? Archie said that, although it was by no means clearcut, he felt that the trustees had, in imposing the undertaking on the new trustees, accepted fiduciary responsibilities towards the transferring members.

"So that brings us to the point," said Colin. "What should we do? If we do nothing and the company survives another 12 months, the members get nothing out of the surplus. If we lend the company the surplus and it goes bust, we will end up in court. Plus we'll have trouble with the new employer-related investment regulations. But if we enforce the conditions and the company goes under, the members will get the surplus but lose their jobs. They're not going to thank us for that, are they?"

"It's all quite simple," said Archie. "We should do a deal. Half a loaf is better than no bread. That way everybody gets a slice of the cake."

The next step was a meeting with the new company's finance director and managing director, who said they were the trustees of the new scheme. All Archie's efforts to persuade them to do a deal failed. The sticking point was an immediate need for £7 million. Nothing less would do. Rather mysteriously they said they had been advised that this was in order; the only obstacle was the protective conditions. And so deadlock was reached. The meeting broke off with a feeling of frustration on both sides.

A few weeks later the phone rang. It was Colin:

"Archie, you gave the right advice after all. The new company has gone down the tube. The loan would simply have gone to repay loans to the bank. The writing was on the wall. Of course the members have lost their jobs, but the conditions did serve their purpose because the surplus will now be used to augment benefits."

"But," said Archie, "if only we could have done a deal, maybe things might have been different. The trouble arose because the sellers did not identify their objectives clearly. Were they trying to smooth the sale or protect the members?"

"OK," said Colin, "what should have been done?"

"Well," said Archie, "if you want to give a management buy out a soft landing, sell them the business cheap. At least that way you're not fooling yourself.

"Next, if you want to give the transferring members a share of the surplus, make sure it is used for them. The best thing is to spend it on benefit improvements; in that way they get an immediate gain. The alternative is earmarking the surplus in perpetuity. But that way you leave someone else to decide how to spend it. Either way you run the risk of landing the new scheme with two classes of members — the sheep and the goats or the old and the new. The problem will be eased when the Social Security Act requires surpluses to be used for giving guaranteed pension increases. But that won't solve all the problems. I think it is basically unsatisfactory to impose protective conditions with a time limit. It merely fogs the issue. I would pay only a transfer value based on past service reserve and spend the extra beforehand on benefit improvements. That way you won't be deluding anyone, including yourself. Handing over a share of surplus only gets sticky fingers itching.

"And do remember that back of the envelope calculations, even if done by actuaries, are really playing roulette. If you don't give the actuary time to get the abacus out and do the sums properly, at least build some formula into the transfer clause limiting the amount to be transferred."

This discussion took place one Friday evening when Colin, Archie, David and Matt were putting the world to rights down at the pub after work. Archie had been boring them about Bermuda and David and Matt were telling Colin how well they got on when Archie was away. Stung, Archie retorted that in that case he would set up an office in the

Caribbean and run the Pensions Department from a desk on the beach.

"The funny thing is," said David, "that the clients seem to want to see you in person. We do better when you're away but they seem to feel cheated. I can't understand it myself. The way they go on would make you think that Archie was some kind of radio and TV personality."

"So that explains the number of meetings you arranged for me that week after I got back. I've never worked so hard in my life," said Archie.

"We thought it was time you did some proper work for a change instead of swanning off to all these conferences," said David and Matt in unison. "By the way, you're off to Manchester again on Monday on the 7.30 shuttle. Here's the file for you to read over the weekend."

First published in *Pensions Management*, November 1990.

# CHAPTER 20

## Help for the Individual

### Background

The Social Security Act 1990 implemented most of the proposals for reform of occupational pension schemes made by the Occupational Pensions Board in its report *Protecting Pensions*. Many of these relate to giving greater protection to individual members of pension schemes.

### The Pensions Ombudsman

The Act provides for a Pensions Ombudsman who will be able to investigate complaints about maladministration or disputes, whether of fact or law. His decisions will be legally binding; an appeal will be permitted only on questions of law. The Ombudsman will set his own procedure but access is to be free. The Ombudsman will be able to make people give evidence and produce documents. His awards will be enforced like a court order. The Ombudsman will produce an annual report.

Thus for the first time members will have a free and effective method of redressing their grievances. No longer will they be faced by the uncertainty, delay and expense of the High Court. This reform will mean not only that trustees will have to be more careful in carrying out their duties, but that they will have to be able to demonstrate that they have acted fairly and properly.

### The register

The Act also provides for a register of personal and occupational pension schemes to be established. It will offer a tracing service to enable members to investigate and claim their pension rights from their former schemes. The register will be open to public inspection without charge. In time a valuable source of information will become available to help members trace deferred pensions in old schemes.

## The Occupational Pensions Advisory Service

The Occupational Pensions Advisory Service (OPAS) was founded in 1983 to advise members of occupational pension schemes about their rights. The Act enables the Secretary of State for Social Services to fund advisory bodies like OPAS, and he lost no time in announcing that OPAS was to become publicly funded. The role of OPAS has been extended to personal as well as occupational pension schemes. OPAS has a London central office at 11 Belgrave Road, London SW1 2UA but it also operates on a regional basis through a network of voluntary advisers. The services of OPAS are free. A levy is imposed on schemes to pay for the register, the ombudsman and OPAS.

## Independent trustees

If an employer becomes insolvent, an independent trustee of the pension scheme now has to be appointed. An independent trustee, once appointed, cannot be removed until a new employer has taken the place of the old one. The independent trustee's fees are paid by the scheme. If the employer was the sole trustee, as often happens with small schemes, the independent trustee will take over. In other circumstances the independent trustee will act jointly with the other trustees.

The independent trustee must have no interest in the employer's or the scheme's assets and must not be connected with or an associate of the employer. In addition, the independent trustee must not have acted as an adviser to the employer or the other trustees in the previous three years.

Any fiduciary powers, eg about pension increases or disposal of surplus on a winding up of the scheme, whether given by the rules to, the employer or the other trustees, are to be exercised *solely* by the independent trustee.

And so at long last it will no longer be possible for liquidators or receivers, acting on behalf of the creditors, to exercise fiduciary or trust powers and divert surplus away from the members. This is another valuable protection for the rights of members of pension schemes when their company goes into liquidation or receivership.

## Self-investment

For the first time general limits on self-investment or "employer-related investment" have been laid down. The Social Security Act gives the Secretary of State for Social Services power to make regulations limiting investments in employer-related assets. Employer-related assets include:

(a) shares and securities in the employer;

(b) land or property used by the employer;

(c) loans to the employer (including unpaid scheme contributions).

The regulations limit investment in employer-related assets to 5% of the assets of the scheme. The regulations do not apply to schemes which:

(a) have less than 12 members who are all trustees of the scheme; and

(b) have a rule that any decision to invest in employer-related investments has to be agreed in writing by all the members.

This is another area where the Government has stepped in to give greater protection to the rights of individual members.

For an illustration of the way in which trustees, and in particular independent trustees, should look after their members' interests, when their employer is insolvent, see "The Lawyer's Tale: Oiling the Wheels" which follows this chapter.

# The Lawyer's Tale: Oiling the Wheels

The collapse of Policy of Success, a national firm of insurance brokers based in Leeds, was the most spectacular so far in 1991 — the year when the recession really began to bite. The Policy of Success Pension Scheme was administered by the Magnificent Mutual Life Assurance Society. The pension superintendent responsible for the scheme was John Watson, who had an infectious love both of football and pensions. He in turn looked after a team of a dozen or so pension administrators whom he lightly controlled with a two foot ruler.

Unlike the company, the pension scheme had flourished and had a surplus of some £20 million. Its winding up rule required the trustees to use the surplus to augment members' benefits up to Inland Revenue limits. Although the surplus was large, augmentation would absorb it, thus leaving nothing for the liquidator.

John Watson's peace was disturbed one morning by a call from one of the trustees, Dave Morris who said: "John, the liquidator has formed a new company, transferred the greater part of the broking business to it and sold it to a Lithuanian refugee who apparently delights in the name of McGregor. The trustees have been asked to sign a deed changing the principal employer from Policy of Success to Success Assured and changing the trustees to McGregor and two of his pals. I'm coming to London tomorrow so I'll call in and see you about noon to discuss it — OK?"

This was fine by John who, sensing trouble, decided to get advice from Docs Galore, the pensions boutique used by the Magnificent Mutual. He asked first for his old friends Archie Smithers and David but was told that they were away on a tour of Eastern European capitals advising governments about privatising their state pensions.

And so he was put on to Martin Richards. Martin, with Archie, was now largely responsible for Docs Galore. Martin was in his early 30s, six foot nine, with an unruly shock of grey hair. But it was his eyes that riveted people. They exercised a hypnotic effect. He was the idol of the conference circuit and on the Pensions Elementals courses regularly scored more A ratings than all the other speakers put together.

And so at noon the next day John and Dave met Martin at the Docs Galore offices near St Paul's. The contrast between Dave and Martin could not have been greater. Dave was short and tubby and had a Yorkshire accent you could cut with a knife.

Dave started off without preliminary: "Well, young man, this is a proper pickle. There's no way I'll hand over my members' scheme to that Lithuanian runabout and his cronies. Plus, I learnt last night they've bought half our surplus from the liquidator. I'll not have it."

John quickly cut in:

"What I think Dave means is that McGregor agreed to pay, by way of additional consideration, 50% of the surplus. It's all set out in the pensions schedule. The actuarial assumptions are all there. The surplus is valued as at 1 January 1991. An amount equal to 50% then has to be paid by five equal annual instaments."

"That's what I said," said Dave. "I only learnt this when I told McGregor that before I signed the deed I wanted him to agree to :
— continue the scheme in its present form;
— have a majority of member representative trustees;
— guarantee LPI pension increases for all service;
— introduce equal pension ages; and
— for good measure spend half of the surplus left over after LPI and equal pension ages on benefit improvements for *all* classes of members — with special emphasis on those made or about to be made redundant."

"What did he say?" asked Martin.

"It was then he told me about the deal with the liquidator. £10 million of our surplus has gone out of the window. LPI would, so the actuary says, cost £5 million. As for equalising pension ages, it's all a mess. But the worst possible interpretation of *Barber* would cost about £7 million. So all he was prepared to do at the moment until LPI becomes law and *Barber* is clarified is to:
— increase the life assurance cover from twice salary to four times; and
— give the active members a 5% service credit with the option of taking a six month contribution holiday, if they prefer it.

"And so I told him to take a running jump back to Riga. We all know *Barber* applies to future service. The NAPF has said so. I told him —

just because we live in Leeds, we don't wear woad — we're not pig
ignorant. Plus I want something for the pensioners and the early
leavers."

John smiled as the tale unfolded.

"So it's all quite simple really, Martin. Just tell us that McGregor
can't make Dave sign the deed. Apparently the other two trustees have
already signed."

"Well," said Martin, "it's all very difficult. I think we need counsel's
opinion and so I've arranged a consultation this afternoon with Sir
Obadiah Thom QC. We'll go along together and see him."

"Counsel," said John. "Archie and Dave don't go to counsel. They
give you the answer there and then."

"Yes," replied Martin with a breezy laugh. "But there's no guarantee
that they give you the right answer, is there? Besides there's all this
new legislation about indpendent trustees and the *Imperial* case.
Life's got very complicated."

Two hours later they were ensconced in the chambers of Sir
Obadiah Thom. It was a large room overlooking the gardens of
Lincoln's Inn. The crocuses were out and the grass was being cut.

Martin began by explaining what had happened. If he had a fault, it
was that he tended to go on. They all — including Sir Obadiah —
glazed over. No doubt it was the effect of lunch. They shouldn't have
had that second bottle of wine.

Eventually Martin ended:

"The rules say that a change of principal employer or the admission
of a new company to participation in the scheme requires the trustees'
consent. Have they got to give it in these circumstances and can they
be removed, if they don't?"

Sir Obadiah sat up with a start. The room was warm. The prints
lining the walls showed Sir Obadiah in his Cambridge rowing team in
1929 and the piles of dusty books and papers that lay everywhere
contributed to the soporific atmosphere.

"Thank you Mr Richards," he said. "I have read the papers. The
answers to your questions, mutatis mutandis, are:

- There's no longer any need for an independent trustee now that
  a new company, not the insolvent employer, has become the
  members' employer. I think you meant to ask me that.
- The liquidator can't remove the trustees. The *Mettoy* case says
  that the power to appoint and remove trustees is a trust or
  "fiduciary" power. It does not pass to a liquidator whose duties

are to the creditors, not the members.
- The new company does not become the principal employer until approved by the trustees; so it can't remove them.
- The trustees do have a discretion in approving the change. They should find out the facts. As long as they do this and act in good faith, that is that.
- The arrangement between the liquidator and the new company, although related to the size of the scheme's surplus, does not directly affect the pension scheme. It should therefore be ignored by the trustees.
- In the end it's all down to negotiation. The trustees should be careful of pushing out the boat too far. Res ipsa loquitur," he concluded with a twinkle.

With that Sir Obadiah rose to his feet. Little clouds of dust spurted up. The conference was ended.

Outside in the March sunshine Dave was the first to speak:

"What was all that Latin for and how old was that guy? Was there really a rowing print from 1929?"

Martin laughed: "They think the punters like a bit of Latin. It makes it all sound more learned. It helps justify his enormous fees. By the way Sir Obadiah is 80, but there are no flies on him for all that. What he was really saying was that you can within reason press your demands but don't go too far."

A week later John and Dave were in Leeds meeting McGregor in the panelled boardroom of the company. McGregor started off by saying:

"I won't tolerate any more delay about this deed changing the principal employer and trustees. I've bought the company from the liquidator. I've paid for the surplus in the pension scheme. I want my men as the trustees. I don't want to hear any more of this crypto-communist talk from rabble rousers like you two."

"Come now," said John in an effort to pour oil on troubled waters, "let's see what we can agree. First, I take it you agree to continue the scheme in its present form."

"Yes", replied McGregor, "as long as you understand I have the legal right to wind it up if necessary, just like the old company did."

"Fine," said Dave. "Now what about the trustees?"

"Well," said McGregor, "there's me, the finance director and the company secretary. Maybe we could have two more. What about you Dave and one other person nominated by you?"

"Agreed," cut in John quickly before Dave could object. "We can't demand a majority. In practice two out of five will do. The rules require the trustees to act unanimously. Now what about pension ages? We know the problem. But you've got a lot of surplus. I've got a suggestion for you both to consider:

- equalise pension ages at 65 for both sexes;
- permit existing members to retire without any reduction between the ages of 60 and 65;
- permit new members to retire early with the normal reduction;
- and give LPI for all service.

"If *Barber* does turn out for the worst and future instalments of pension have to be equalised, that'll cost you £7 million according to the actuary. As a compromise why don't we wait and see what happens about *Barber*. When we know, we can do the sums again and divvy up the surplus 50:50. In the meantime the trustees would, of course, require you to pay company contributions in full."

McGregor nearly choked on his cigar; words failed him. John quickly seized the initiative again:

"I know you did that deal with the liquidator. But that's nothing to do with us. We'd have told you to shy away from the pension scheme if you'd asked us, but you didn't. Maybe trustees should in future be consulted in advance."

Dave butted in:

"The trustees considered this yesterday. John has told you the terms for our agreeing to sign. If you don't like them, we are in an impossible position. We shall have to apply to the court for guidance on what we as trustees ought to do. I don't imagine the liquidator would like that much.

"Why don't you renegotiate your deal with him. Remind him that the *Imperial Tobacco* case imposed a duty of good faith on employers, remind him that the Court of Session in Scotland decided last summer that receivers owe a duty of care to the company's employees and have to act reasonably towards them. Remind him that he might be viewed, in American parlance, as a plan fiduciary, and to have acted to the profit of the creditors in conflict with his duty to the members. In short remind him that a quarter of a loaf is better than no bread."

First published in *Pensions Management*, March 1991.

# CHAPTER 21

# Increases to Pensions in Payment

## Background

The way in which guaranteed minimum pensions and protected rights pensions are revalued between the member leaving the scheme and State pension age are explained in Chapter 17 "Contracting Out". That chapter also explains how guaranteed minimum pensions and protected rights pensions are revalued when they come into payment at State pension age. Chapter 18 "Preservation" explains how the balance of the deferred pension prospectively payable to an early leaver (that is the excess over the guaranteed minimum pension or protected rights pension) is revalued between the date of the member leaving the scheme and his or her reaching normal retirement date.

## Limited price indexation

The Social Security Act 1990 completes the picture by introducing requirements for pensions, once they come into payment, to be revalued. Guaranteed minimum pensions and money purchase benefits are excluded. Pensions in payment will in future have to be revalued in line with the Retail Prices Index up to a maximum of 5% — limited price indexation or LPI. The relevant parts of the Act will bite in two stages.

Firstly, all pensions attributable to service after a day still to be appointed (but unlikely to be before April 1992) will have to be revalued in this way.

Secondly, if the scheme's actuarial valuation shows a surplus, the surplus must be used to provide limited price indexation for all service before the appointed day. All classes of members — active members, deferred pensioners as well as current pensioners — will benefit from this, when their pensions come into payment. If the surplus is not big enough, the trustees may be given a discretion to use it for pension increases on an age-related basis. For example, the trustees might be permitted to use all the surplus on indexation for current pensioners, leaving active members and deferred pensioners to catch up later from future surpluses. But apart from this the surplus must be applied rateably among all classes of members.

The basis for calculating surplus for this purpose has not yet been fixed but draft guidance notes have been produced by the Institute and Faculty of Actuaries which indicate that surplus will be calculated using the scheme's normal actuarial methods and assumptions. It may be that this part of the Act relating to past service indexation will be postponed until the *Barber* decision has been clarified and schemes are able to calculate their precise liabilities. Chapter 13 "Equal Treatment" explains the areas of uncertainty in the *Barber* judgement.

It is the Government's intention that surplus will not be available for any purpose, including a refund of surplus, contribution holidays or benefit improvements, until LPI for all past service has been guaranteed. Already payments to an employer out of the scheme's resources are, with certain minor exceptions, prohibited until LPI has been guaranteed; and this is the case whether the scheme is ongoing or winding up.

## Discretionary pension increases

It is important to remember that even where LPI has been fully implemented, scheme rules will usually give the trustees, with the employer's agreement, a discretionary power to award increases on top. To what extent trustees feel able to make use of such a discretion will depend on the level of price inflation, the resources of the scheme and the employer's consent.

For an illustration of the way in which LPI for past service works in practice, see "The Lawyer's Tale: Spanner in the Works" which follows this chapter.

# The Lawyer's Tale:
# Spanner in the Works

Ever since the Magnificent Mutual Life Assurance Society had privatised its documents department, its work had flourished. Under its new name of Docs Galore, Archie Smithers and his assistant young David had got busier and busier. First of all they had taken on a young lawyer called Matt and recently they had recruited a trainee named Rod. Even with doubling their numbers it was a struggle to cope.

Archie had been consulted by Colonel Braithwaite of Braithwaite Precision Engineering about two pension schemes they inherited on a takeover of two associated companies last year. Both companies had their own schemes. One was in surplus to the extent of £1.5 million, while the other had a deficit of £250,000, plus arrears of company contributions amounting to a further £250,000. Colonel Braithwaite rang up Archie and said:

"I want to write off the company arrears in the Nuts and Bolts Scheme and merge it with the Widgets Scheme. That will use up £500,000 of the Widgets surplus. I can run off the rest in about 18 months with a company contribution holiday. Then when the Nuts and Bolts Scheme has been merged and the Widgets Scheme is in balance, I'll pop it into the Braithwaite Scheme. I take it that doesn't give rise to any problems. The actuary, Colin Bell, is suggesting that the trustees get independent legal advice. Can't see the point myself."

"Well," said Archie, "who are the trustees?"

"That's easy," replied the Colonel, "I replaced the trustees who were there at the time of the takeover with myself, our company secretary and my own secretary, Miss Midge. So there'll be no problem. Just get one of your chaps to give the trustees the all clear."

Archie gave the file to David. After he had read it he spoke to Archie:

"It's not so easy as you made it out, Archie. I don't see how we can give the trustees clearance. If I write and tell the Colonel that, it will make you look an idiot and the Colonel will go wild."

"Calm yourself," replied Archie. "Let's start with the Nuts and Bolts Scheme. The trustees of that scheme want to ensure that their members get transferred to the Widgets Scheme with mirror image benefits. If they can get the Widgets trustees to agree to give year for year past service benefits, then the Nuts and Bolts trustees can:

— agree to the transfer, and

— waive the arrears of company contributions."

"But why should the Widgets trustees agree?" asked David, adding, "It doesn't help that they are one and the same people."

"The answer," said Archie, "is that the Widgets trustees have got no control over the admission of new members or over a participating company. The trick in these situations is to distinguish matters which need the trustees' consent and those which don't. The Widgets trustees are not required to give their consent to Nuts and Bolts participating in their scheme."

"But," said David, "that doesn't help. It will only give the Nuts and Bolts members benefits for future service. They'd be idiots if they gave them full past service benefits - the transfer payment would not cover it. If the company is let off the hook of paying its arrears, there will be a deficit of £500,000."

"Well," said Archie, "if I were the Colonel, I would ask the Widgets trustees to exercise their discretion and use part of the Widgets surplus to augment the Nuts and Bolts members' benefits. I would remind them that if they did not feel minded to do this, the company might well not be minded to go on paying contributions."

"But," cried David, "that's blackmail, plus the Widgets company is taking a contribution holiday already."

"I know," replied Archie, "but if the Widgets company indicated that it would *not* pay any more contributions, the trustees would be in a mess. Sooner or later the surplus would run out and they'd have to wind up the scheme."

"You are a crafty old devil, Archie," said David with a grin.

"Not really," said Archie. "It's just a matter of explaining things in the right light!"

And so the letter of advice was dispatched. This was all at the beginning of March.

It was lovely and warm that weekend and Archie was sitting in the garden in his deckchair reading the *Financial Times*. He had done a good morning's work and was relaxing over a bottle of Australian Chardonnay. Suddenly he leapt out of his chair with a shriek. Now the *Financial Times* doesn't usually produce such an electric effect on its readers.

What had upset Archie was the announcement that not only was the Government going to introduce guaranteed pension increases in line with the Retail Prices Index with a limit of 5% for all future service, but that if a scheme had a surplus, the first call on the surplus was to give guaranteed pension increases for past service. What's more a company could not get round this by taking a refund of surplus or a contribution holiday.

Archie waited for the amendments to the Social Security Bill to come out and then wrote to the Colonel saying that this put an end to the merger. The Colonel rang up in a fury and demanded a meeting. And this is where life got very unfair. The Colonel was so beside himself with rage that he refused to meet Archie.

"Get me someone competent," he cried. "Not some old has-been who doesn't keep up with what's going on."

This was a little unjust but the Colonel and Archie had never seen eye to eye. Young David was the Colonel's favourite. But David was just off on his annual holiday.

"Send someone else then," thundered the Colonel. "Anyone so long as it's not you!"

The upshot was that Matt was left in the lurch to sort out the mess. He was terrified of the Colonel but knew that there was no alternative but to go to the meeting. As moral support he took with him the new trainee, Rod. And so three days later they sat down with Colonel Braithwaite in his panelled boardroom with the Widgets actuary, Colin Bell. Matt had been worried sick about the meeting and his worries were compounded when he met Rod at the station *en route* to the Colonel. Rod was wearing a light grey silver suit and grey shoes and over his suit he wore a psychedelic ski jacket in dayglo orange and pink. But it was Rod's tie that made the difference between success and disaster. It was a sober regimental tie and the regiment, by a happy coincidence, was the Colonel's.

The Colonel spotted Rod's tie immediately, and greeted Rod like a long lost friend.

Matt explained that the original letter of advice was quite correct when it was written but it had got overtaken by events. The effect of the amendments to the Social Security Bill was that the Widgets surplus became earmarked for the Widgets members to give them guaranteed pension increases for their past service.

"But this is changing the goal posts and swapping horses mid-stream," cried the Colonel mixing metaphors in his excitement. He went on: "I knew this lot in power were a bunch of closet commies. What ever will they do next?"

"Nay, don't take on so," said Colin, in broad Northern tones. "It all depends on what you mean by a surplus. There've got to be regulations and the Government is having discussions with the Institute of Actuaries. Plus it's not even law yet. It's not even planned to come into force until 1992. Don't get so over-excited, Matt. We'll press a few buttons on the calculator next year and make the surplus go away. Just leave it to me, Colonel."

"It's not so simple," replied Matt. "It's no use pretending you can do the impossible next year. It's this year you've got to worry about. How can the Widgets trustees agree to use part of their surplus now to augment past service benefits for the Nuts and Bolts members and waive the company's arrears of contributions when Parliament has as good as said that that surplus is earmarked for pension increases. As soon as the Widgets members find out, the trustees would be done for breach of trust. They would not be acting in the interests of their members. And it doesn't make my job any easier with them being the same trustees for the two schemes. And what's more, you ought to get some independent trustees - not just yourself, Colonel, and a couple of stooges."

"Well, young man," said the Colonel, "as you know I don't like advisers who cause difficulties. But for once I am impressed. Now that I have taken on board that my hard earned money in the Widgets scheme can be taken from me, what you say makes sense. Well, as the owner of Nuts and Bolts, I am not going to stump up the arrears of company contributions. So what should I do?"

"Mmm," said Colin, "what about me having a go at the Nuts and Bolts actuary to see if I can't persuade him to change some of his assumptions? As you know, I advised you last year when you took over Nuts and Bolts that the valuation was very conservative and it was a couple of years out of date."

At this point Rod could contain himself no longer. His voice cracking with excitement he cried: "Don't change the assumptions - change the actuary. It's obvious!"

"If," continued Rod, "you were the Nuts and Bolts actuary, Colin, would there be a £250,000 deficit?"

"No, Rod," replied Colin, "I could, if pressed, even produce a bit of a surplus."

"£250,000 of surplus — that sort of thing!" asked Rod.

"Well, I'd have to have a think about it but give or take the odd pound, I think I could make it about that. I did explain all this to you last year, Colonel. You said you paid for the Widgets surplus but you didn't in fact. We simply took the Nuts and Bolts deficit and the Widgets surplus and said they cancelled each other out. The other side fell for it and you got a bargain. But there's still a problem — I'm not the Nuts and Bolts actuary."

"He will be shortly, won't he, Colonel," said Rod.

"Eh, Rod, you can't play fast and loose with actuaries. We're not like monkeys, you know!"

"I think," said Rod, "that a phone call between such important professional people should sort things out. Something along the lines of — either the scheme changes its actuarial assumptions or it changes its actuary. That should do the trick. Of course I know you'll dress it up in pretty language but if he's not thick, he'll understand. And if he is thick, you need a new actuary!"

"Bravo," said Colonel Braithwaite. "Am I right - if there's no deficit and enough surplus to wipe out the arrears of contributions, we are home and dry?"

"Yes," replied Matt, "because then the Widgets trustees don't have to give their consent to anything. There's enough money in the Nuts and Bolts Scheme for a full actuarial transfer payment. The Widgets trustees could hardly refuse the transfer in those circumstances and their consent to the admission of the Nuts and Bolts company to the Widgets Scheme isn't required.

"You're home and dry. The company contribution holiday, given the enlarged membership, will eliminate the surplus before 1992."

"Bring out the champagne, Miss Midge," said the Colonel, "and let's celebrate."

First published in *Pensions Management*, July 1990.

# CHAPTER 22

# Who Owns a Pension Scheme's Surplus?

## Background

Many final salary schemes are showing a healthy surplus. This has led to renewed interest in the question of who owns that surplus. Employers usually assume it is theirs as they are expected to pay the balance of cost in a final salary scheme, but members often feel that money in a pension fund is there for the purpose of providing pensions. There have been a number of cases on this subject. Most of the cases have lent support to the view that the surplus effectively belongs to the employer.

## The *Hillsdown* case

The question to be decided here was whether a bulk transfer payment from one scheme to another on the sale of a company should include a share of the surplus. The judge, Walton J, said that a surplus had no existence in reality but was "what may be termed temporary surplus funding by the employing company". There was no certainty that the surplus, if transferred, would be used for the members' benefit. And so he refused to order that the transfer payment should include a share of the surplus.

## The *Courage* case

In this case the judge's observations on the ownership of surplus are even more encouraging to employers. He also saw surpluses as arising from what, with hindsight, is past over-funding. He said that any surplus arises from past over-funding not in proportion to the employer's and the members' contributions but by the employer alone to the full extent of its past contributions. However, having said that members have no legal right to participate in the surplus of a continuing scheme, the judge, Millett J, went on to say that they were entitled to have it dealt with by negotiation and consultation with their employers and trustees and not to be irrevocably parted from it by the unilateral decision of a takeover raider. So members have a right to be considered in relation to a surplus.

# The winding up cases

Next come three decisions on the ownership of surplus on the winding up of a scheme. This turns on the winding up rule. What it says on the subject will decide the issue. The trouble is that many winding up rules were vaguely and ambiguously drafted at a time when surpluses were not much in evidence.

### *The* Icarus *case*

The company went into liquidation and the pension scheme was wound up. The rules gave the company discretion to use the surplus to increase benefits. Any balance went back to the company. The judge, Aldous J, found that the surplus largely arose from good investment. If the company had continued, it could have taken a contribution holiday and so he concluded that the surplus was due to overfunding by the company. The liquidator, as long as he acted in good faith and considered all the facts, could pay the surplus to the creditors and use none for the members. The case therefore bears out the conventional view that a pension surplus is an employer's asset.

### *The* Mettoy *case*

Here the facts were similar to those in *Icarus*. Again, the company had a discretion to use surplus on winding up for the benefit of the members. The judge, Warner J, decided that this discretion, although vested in the company, was a fiduciary or trust power. It could not, therefore, be exercised by a liquidator or receiver because of the impossible conflict of interest between the members and the creditors. In the circumstances the judge would have to exercise the discretion.

The judge stressed that the members were not volunteers. They earned their pension in the same way as their pay. He did not think it was correct to say that members' rights were satisfied when they had received the benefits laid down by the rules, and that anything more lay in the bounty of the company. "One cannot in my view in construing a provision in the rules of a balance of cost pension scheme relating to surplus, start from an assumption that any surplus belongs morally to the employer." But tantalisingly he did not go on to say that surplus belongs morally to the members. The *Mettoy* case is about to be appealed.

### Davis v Richards & Wallington

This was an unusual case because the scheme had been set up on interim documentation. When it came to be wound up there was no winding up rule. The judge, Scott J, decided that the surplus belonged to the company because it was liable to pay the balance of cost. It was likely that all of the surplus arose from company contributions. The members paid defined contributions in return for defined benefits. This reasoning is hard to follow and contrasts sharply with the *Mettoy* case where Warner J said that members were not just entitled to receive defined benefits but had a moral claim to be considered in the distribution of the surplus.

In circumstances such as these an independent trustee now has to be appointed. The independent trustee is alone competent to exercise fiduciary powers, whether vested in the company or the other trustees. In addition, surplus must now be used to provide limited price indexation for all service; only any balance remaining after that will be subject to the trustees' discretion or returned to the company, or whatever the winding up rule provides.

### The *Imperial Tobacco Pension Fund* case

The Imperial Tobacco pension fund gave guaranteed increases to pensions in payment of 5% or in line with the Retail Prices Index, if less. The trustees could amend the scheme rules with the company's consent. The judge, Sir Nicolas Browne-Wilkinson, decided that the power of the company to consent was not a fiduciary power, but the

company was nevertheless bound to consider proposals for amendment and could not state in advance that it would not consent in the
future.

In considering whether or not to give its consent, the company was
bound to give effect to the implied duty to maintain mutual trust and
confidence on the part of both the employee and the employer. There
was therefore to be implied in the pension scheme a provision that the
company would not conduct itself in a manner likely to destroy the
relationship of trust and confidence between it and the members.

This is another ruling that pension benefits are "pay" in line with
the *Mettoy* case and also with the European case of *Barber v Guardian
Royal Exchange* (dealt with in Chapter 13). While the judgement (like
that in the *Courage* case) indicates that members have a right not to be
parted from "their surplus", it does not give them a right to the
surplus. Like the *Mettoy* judgement there are indications (but no
more) that surplus does not necessarily belong to the company, but the
judge refrained from deciding who does own it. Again, the judge
stressed that members had earned their rights. But it is clear
nevertheless that a company can act in its own self-interest, although
it cannot act capriciously nor for an ulterior motive, for example to take
back a surplus to which it is not otherwise entitled. In particular, the
judgement does not require surpluses to be used for pension increases
or benefit improvements. There is nothing to stop a company from
taking a contribution holiday. But the case will make it much harder
for a company to extract surplus from a pension scheme otherwise
than by way of a contribution holiday.

# Conclusion

So where do these cases leave employers and trustees? The indications
are that judges will look closely at the factors that led to the surplus —
investment performance, redundancies, employer's and members'
contributions. At this stage it is impossible to draw firm conclusions,
particularly from the cases about the winding up of a scheme. In a
continuing scheme members can still expect to earn further benefits,
while in the winding up cases the members had lost their jobs.
Furthermore, only on a winding up does a surplus really exist. Before
then it is only an actuarial estimate. It is likely, therefore, that in
ongoing schemes the courts will lean to viewing surpluses as arising

from past overfunding by the company. On winding up, it all depends on what the rules say.

Where trustees are faced with requests by an employer for a refund of surplus from an ongoing scheme, they have to act in the interests of the members. They have to consider the balance of power as between them and the company, as set out in the trust deed and rules. They must consider what will happen if they refuse the company's request; they may lose the company's goodwill which is essential for the continued running of the scheme. In these circumstances they have a duty to bargain with the employer and to seek the best deal they can for their members.

For an illustration of the way in which these problems are dealt with see "The Lawyer's Tale : A Salve for Insolvency" which follows this chapter.

# The Lawyer's Tale:
# A Salve for Insolvency

Maud Blenkinsop sat alone in her teak panelled office in the Isle of Dogs. She was the last of the Blenkinsops in J.Blenkinsop & Daughter (Ironfounders) Limited. But the yuppies and the Taiwanese had beaten her. The yuppies had put an inflated value on her island freehold, which, as her boring accountant nephews unfailingly reminded her, meant she would make more by selling up and investing the proceeds. The Taiwanese undercut the Japanese, let alone J. Blenkinsop & Daughter. Shrewdly, on the advice of her pensions consultant, Roger Davenport from the Magnificent Mutual Life Assurance Society, she had sold the freehold years ago to the Blenkinsop Pension Scheme.

The company belonged equally to Maud and her three nephews. They were not wildly enthusiastic when, at the ripe young age of 73, Maud threw in the towel.

"If I go under now," she told Roger, "at least the company will be able to pay its debts. But I will have the satisfaction of seeing off my nephews with nothing to show for their shares."

"But what about your shareholding?" asked Roger.

"Well, that's gone down the tube as well. But the men can all get other jobs quite easily. They won't lose out. And I am a rich woman in my own right. Plus the pension scheme is stuffed with cash. At any rate, the only ones to go down the tube are me and my nephews. I am quite happy to cut off my nose to spite their faces. They're all rolling in money and have the most boring wives and disagreeable children."

Roger thought it was time to bring Maud to order.

"So the company is going into liquidation and it should be able to pay off the creditors. But there'll be nothing left over for the shareholders. Colin Bell, our actuary, says the pension scheme will be able to pay full Revenue limits pensions for everyone, based on all company service — not just pensionable service — plus index-linked pensions. However, it does depend on the trustees deciding to augment benefits; if they don't, the members just get their early leavers benefits."

"I know that," said Maud, "which is why I never had outside trustees. I am the sole trustee and I will augment benefits in full."

"But," interjected Roger, "you aren't the trustee. The company is."

"Stop quibbling," said Maud. "I am the company."

Roger decided that nothing was to be gained from arguing. "Let's go to lunch," he said.

"Yes," said Maud looking longingly at Roger. Roger was tall and handsome and had a mass of blonde curly hair. He wore a fashionable double-breasted grey suit and black suede shoes. Two weeks later she met Roger again. This was because the liquidator of the company had called on her and said that he wanted to talk about the pension scheme and its surplus. And so Maud arranged a meeting with Roger to be followed by a meeting with the liquidator.

Roger sensed trouble and therefore arranged to see the actuary, Colin Bell, and Archie Smithers, the Magnificent Mutual's lawyer, because he was sure there would be legal complications.

Colin explained that on winding up the scheme would have a surplus of about £5 million. He could just about use it all up if the trustees granted full benefit improvements.

"So that's fine by me," Colin said. "End of problem except that Archie's face looks so miserable he must be about to put a spanner in the works."

"I'm afraid I am," said Archie. "I have to make a confession. You may remember, Roger, that the Blenkinsop scheme was one we took over from the Megabuck and Megalopolitan about ten years ago."

"Yes, I do remember," replied Roger. "I had just started with the Magnificent Mutual and Blenkinsops were my first scheme. Old Maudie has always had a soft spot for me."

"Now we know why you have those three hour lunches with her once a month," said Colin.

Roger's suede shoes twitched with embarrassment but he quickly recovered himself and said: "Well, what of it Archie?".

"The problem," said Archie, "is that I changed the rules. The scheme had had no rule changes since 1969. New code requirements, preservation, equal access, contracting out and numerous benefit improvements had all been affected by announcements. So I did a new set of rules based on our standard. Our winding up rule gives the company, not the trustees, the discretionary power to use surplus on winding up to augment benefits. The old rules gave this power to the trustees. Since the company is now in liquidation, it is the liquidator who will exercise this power. His duty is to the creditors and shareholders, not the members. And so he's not going to augment the benefits, is he?"

"Eh, Archie, why did you do this?" asked Colin in horror.

"The reason is simple. My boss, the senior pensions actuary, is an employer's man. He believes that defined benefits mean what they say. And so any discretion has to be given to the company, not the trustees. I don't happen to agree. But you know what it's like working in a documents department. You can't even sneeze without an actuarial certificate," Archie ended lamely.

"But you shouldn't have done it without telling someone. You can't just go round upsetting the balance of power without so much as a by-your-leave," growled Colin.

"Oh I know you're right," replied Archie, "but it's done all the time."

And so a full team called on Maud the next day. As well as Roger and Colin there was Archie and his assistant, David. It was well known that Maud could not stand Archie. But David being young and good looking was another of Maud's favourites.

When they all turned up at ten o'clock, there was consternation. Maud had only booked a lunch table for four, namely herself, Roger, Colin and David. She smiled condescendingly at Archie, saying:

"I had no idea you were gracing us with your presence. But as you're such a busy man, I expect you'll want to leave immediately after the meeting." David tried hard not to grin.

Archie explained the full story to Maud and said that the liquidator would claim the surplus for the shareholders.

"How could you have done this to me? If my nephews collar the surplus, it will kill me," said Maud. She seemed to swell in her rage as she towered over Archie, brandishing a paper knife.

"Take it easy, Maud," said Roger quickly. "I think I may be able to help. David, wasn't there some case recently that you told me about last week when I gave you a lift to cricket?"

"Yes," said David. "It's the *Mettoy* case, but we'd better get Archie to explain."

"What case?" said Archie. "I don't remember it. I've been going to a lot of conferences recently and I haven't had time to read all the magazine articles that come out. They're written by layabouts with nothing better to do."

"Well here goes," said David. "The Mettoy company — you remember they used to make Corgi cars — went bust. Their pension scheme had a large surplus and the company was given the power to use it to augment benefits on a wind up. But, just like the Blenkinsop scheme, the rules had been changed without telling anyone. The old rules had given this power to the trustees. The new ones gave it to the company. The judge didn't take too kindly to that."

"Do get to the point," said Archie testily. "We don't want to give Maud a long-winded explanation, do we?"

"Well," said David, "the judge said that, although the power had been transferred from the trustees to the company, it was still a fiduciary power. It was for that reason that the amendment was valid. The power couldn't be exercised by the liquidator, because of the conflict of interest. The judge said that he would exercise the power himself and called upon the trustees, the members and the liquidator to give him their suggestions. But reading between the lines my guess is that precious little will go to the creditors."

"Oh David, that's such a relief," said Maud. "You must come and stay with me in my villa at Cap d'Antibes when all this is over. I would ask you, Roger, but you're married and I have no spare room for a married couple. Of course — if you could come alone!"

Thus prepared they met with the liquidator. He explained that the company was just about solvent but that he owed it to the shareholders to realise the company's assets as profitably as he could. One of these was the surplus in the pension scheme. A recent case had established that, whereas here the company was the sole trustee, the liquidator had to exercise his powers in a fiduciary way. But there was nothing to stop him giving nothing to the members, and everything to the creditors or shareholders so long as he had considered all the relevant facts and reached his decision honestly and responsibly.

"Oh yes, I know. That's the *Icarus* case," said David. "But it's not as good as the *Mettoy* case which I have just been telling everyone about. For a start, it's only 11 pages long. *Mettoy* is 130."

"You don't measure the worth of cases by the yard," said the liquidator.

"No, but it tells you something," said David. "I don't think the *Icarus* case was properly argued. Maybe the judge in *Mettoy* went over the top but no stone was left unturned. Besides which I like the *Mettoy* decision. I don't like *Icarus*; I'm not trying to get into an argument about who owns surplus. The judge was careful to avoid that but he did say:

'One cannot, in my opinion, in construing a provision in the rules of a balance of cost pension scheme relating to surplus, start from an assumption that any surplus belongs morally to the employer.'

"And so, to sum it all up, my feeling is that judges in future will follow the *Mettoy* decision rather than *Icarus*. Since in this case there are no creditors, only shareholders, I think the judge will give the money to the members. So I'd back off, if I were you," he concluded triumphantly.

"Bravo," said Maud. Turning to the liquidator she ordered him to leave. "I know my nephews don't like litigation; they don't like paying anyone, let alone lawyers. So you'd better run away without my surplus." As she left the room she turned to Archie:

"I am amazed that the Magnificent Mutual employ a superannuated old goat like you. You don't keep up to date with the new developments and you alter my rules without even asking me. If it hadn't been for David, my men would have been down the tube."

Three hours later, Roger, Colin and David got back to the office after a lunch that was spectacular even by Maud's standards.

Colin and Roger left David to face Archie alone.

"Congratulations, David," he smiled. "You did a first class job. I'm sorry I let you down. Thank goodness you saved the day. It just goes to show we'll have to be a lot more careful now than we used to be about junking old rules and replacing them with our standard."

"I agree," replied David, "but when the Social Security Bill becomes law Maud's problem will be partially solved because:

— if the company is insolvent, an independent trustee will have to be appointed to act alongside the existing trustees; and
— pensions in payment and in deferment will have to be revalued in line with prices up to a ceiling of 5%, before any surplus can be paid to the company.

"But I did think that Maud aged 73 calling you a superannuated old goat was a bit rich!"

First published in *Pensions Management*, May 1990.

# CHAPTER 23

# Principles of Trusteeship

In their report "Protecting Pensions" the Occupational Pensions Board recommended that a brief statement of the principles of trusteeship should be prepared and that the disclosure requirements should be extended to include information about whether each trustee has received a copy of the statement. The following principles, which are not an official statement, have been prepared for that purpose.

1. Trustees must carry out their duties as honest and prudent people would in their own affairs. A higher standard of diligence and knowledge is expected from paid trustees.
2. Trustees must act in the best interests of their beneficiaries and not obtain any personal benefit for themselves.
3. Trustees must act impartially between all classes of beneficiaries.
4. Trustees must not delegate their duties except where permitted by law or scheme rules.
5. Trustees must make themselves familiar with their trust deed and rules, the scheme's investments and other relevant matters.
6. Trustees must obtain and consider expert advice in areas where they are not themselves expert.
7. Trustees must take steps to collect all money owing to the scheme.
8. Trustees must hold the scheme assets for the benefit of the beneficiaries and not pay benefits to other persons.
9. Trustees must record the transactions and proceedings of the scheme.
10. Trustees must keep and be ready with proper accounts of the trust property.

The official statement is being prepared by the Occupational Pensions Board but was not available at the time of going to press.

# CHAPTER 24

# Glossary of Terms

This chapter reproduces some of the definitions contained in Pensions Terminology — 3rd edition, published by the Pensions Management Institute and Pensions Research Accounts Group. This reproduction is by the kind permission of the Institute.

**ACCRUED BENEFITS** — The benefits for service up to a given point in time, whether vested rights or not. They may be calculated in relation to current earnings or projected earnings. Allowance may also be made for revaluation and/or pension increases required by the scheme rules or legislation.

**ACCRUED RIGHTS** — A term sometimes used to describe accrued benefits. The term is given specific definitions for the purposes of preservation, contracting out and the Disclosure Regulations.

**ACTUARIAL ASSUMPTIONS** — The set of assumptions as to rates of return, inflation, increase in earnings, mortality etc, used by the actuary in an actuarial valuation or other actuarial calculations.

**ACTUARIAL DEFICIENCY** — The excess of the actuarial liability over the actuarial value of assets on the basis of the valuation method used. If an actuarial report refers to a surplus or deficiency, it must be studied to ascertain precisely what assets and liabilities have been taken into account. In a stricter sense, the terms surplus and deficiency might be used in relation to the results of a discontinuance valuation.

**ACTUARIAL SURPLUS** — The excess of the actuarial value of assets over the actuarial liability on the basis of the valuation method used. See notes under actuarial deficiency.

**ACTUARIAL VALUATION** — An investigation by an actuary into the ability of a pension scheme to meet its liabilities. This is usually to assess the funding level and a recommended contribution rate based on comparing the actuarial value of assets and the actuarial liability.

**ADDED YEARS** — The provision of extra pension benefits by reference to an additional period of pensionable service in a defined benefit scheme, arising from the receipt of a transfer payment, the paying of additional voluntary contributions or by way of augmentation.

**ADDITIONAL VOLUNTARY CONTRIBUTIONS** — Contributions over and above a member's normal contributions, if any, which a member elects to pay to the scheme in order to secure additional benefits. See also free standing additional voluntary contributions.

**APPROPRIATE PERSONAL PENSION SCHEME** — A personal pension scheme or free standing AVC scheme granted an appropriate scheme certificate by the OPB, enabling its members to use it for the purpose of contracting out.

**AUGMENTATION** — The provision of additional benefits in respect of particular members, normally where the cost is borne by the pension scheme and/or the employer.

**BULK TRANSFER** — The transfer of a group of members from one pension scheme to another, usually with a transfer payment in respect of their accrued benefits under the first scheme. The SFO should be consulted about any such transfer payments.

**BUY BACK** — A term used to describe the payment of a type of state scheme premium by means of which a member's rights are fully reinstated under SERPS.

**BUY OUT** — The purchase by pension scheme trustees of an insurance policy or bond in the name of the beneficiary, in lieu of entitlement to benefit from the scheme.

**CASH EQUIVALENT** — The amount which a member of a pension scheme may under schedule 1A of the Social Security Pensions Act 1975, require to be applied as a transfer payment to another permitted pension scheme or to a buy out policy.

**CENTRALISED SCHEME** — A pension scheme operated on behalf of several employers.

**COMMUTATION** — The giving up of a part or all of the pension payable from retirement for an immediate cash sum.

**CONTRACTED-OUT REBATE** — The amount by which National Insurance contributions in respect of upper band earnings are reduced in respect of employees who are contracted out by virtue of their membership of an occupational pension scheme. The term is also commonly used to describe the equivalent payment made by the DSS as minimum contributions to a personal pension scheme.

**CONTRIBUTION HOLIDAY** — A period during which employers' and/or members' contributions are temporarily suspended, normally when the fund is in surplus. The term is sometimes used loosely when contributions continue to be paid but at a reduced rate.

**DEFERRED PENSIONER** — A person entitled to preserved benefits. Sometimes referred to as a deferred member. The term is also sometimes used to describe a member on postponed retirement.

**DEFINED BENEFIT SCHEME** — A pension scheme in which the rules specify the benefits to be paid, and the scheme is financed accordingly.

**DEFINED CONTRIBUTION SCHEME** — An alternative term for a money purchase scheme, normally one where the rate of contribution is specified in the rules.

**DEPENDANT** — A person who is financially dependent on a member or pensioner or was so at the time of death or retirement of the member or pensioner. For SFO purposes a spouse qualifies automatically as a dependant and a child of the member or pensioner may always be regarded as a dependant until attaining the age of 18 or ceasing to receive full-time educational or vocational training, if later.

**DISCONTINUANCE VALUATION** — An actuarial valuation carried out to assess the position if the scheme were to be discontinued and the trustees were to wind it up in accordance with the requirements of the trust instrument. The valuation may take into account the possible exercise of any discretion to augment benefits.

**DYNAMISATION/DYNAMISM** — A term sometimes used to describe escalation or indexation. It is also used to describe index linking of earnings, either for calculating scheme benefits, or for determining final remuneration for the purpose of SFO limitations.

**EARLY LEAVER** — A person who ceases to be an active member of a pension scheme, other than on death, without being granted an immediate retirement benefit.

**ESCALATION** — A system whereby pensions in payment and/or preserved benefits are automatically increased at regular intervals and at a fixed percentage rate. The percentage may be restricted to the increase in a specified index.

**EX GRATIA BENEFIT** — A benefit provided by the employer which he or she is neither legally nor contractually required to provide.

**EXEMPT APPROVED SCHEME** — An approved scheme other than a personal pension scheme which is established under irrevocable trusts (or exceptionally, subject to a formal direction under s.592(1) of the Income and Corporation Taxes Act 1988) thus giving rise to the tax reliefs specified in the Income and Corporation Taxes Act 1988.

**EXPRESSION OF WISH** — A term used to describe a nomination which is not binding on the trustees.

**FINAL REMUNERATION** — The term used by the SFO for the maximum amount of earnings which it will permit to be used for the purpose of calculating maximum approvable benefits.

**FREE STANDING ADDITIONAL VOLUNTARY CONTRIBUTIONS** — A pension contract separate from a company pension scheme effected by an active member of that scheme. Benefits are secured with a pension provider by contributions from the member only.

**FREE STANDING AVC SCHEME** — A scheme established by a pension provider to accept free standing additional voluntary contributions.

**FUNDING** — The provision in advance for future liabilities by the accumulation of assets, normally external to the employer's business.

**FUNDING PLAN** — The arrangement of the incidence over time of payments with the aim of meeting the future cost of a given set of benefits. Possible objectives of a funding plan might be that, if the actuarial assumptions are borne out by events:

(a) A specified funding level should be reached by a given date.

(b) The level of contributions should remain constant, or should after a planned period be the standard contribution rate required by the valuation method used in the actuarial valuation.

**GUARANTEED MINIMUM PENSION** — The minimum pension which an occupational pension scheme (other than a money purchase contracted-out scheme) must provide as one of the conditions of contracting out. For an employee contracted out under any occupational or personal pension scheme, an amount equal to this amount is deducted from his or her benefit under the state scheme.

**INDEXATION** — A system whereby pensions in payment and/or preserved benefits are automatically increased at regular intervals and by reference to a specified index of prices or earnings. The term is also occasionally used in relation to index linking of final pensionable earnings or final remuneration: see explanation under dynamisation.

**INTEGRATION** — The design of pension scheme benefits to take into account all or part of the state scheme benefits which the member is deemed to receive. One form of integration involves a state pension disregard.

**LOWER EARNINGS LIMIT** — The minimum amount, approximately equivalent to the basic component, which must be earned in any pay period before contributions become payable to the state scheme. Once the limit is exceeded, contributions are payable in respect of earnings both above and below this limit.

**MANAGED FUND** — An investment contract by means of which an insurance company offers participation in one or more pooled funds. Sometimes also used to denote an arrangement where the scheme assets are invested on similar lines to unit trusts by an external investment manager.

**MEMBER** — A person who has been admitted to membership of a pension scheme and is entitled to benefit under the scheme. Sometimes used to refer only to an active member. For some statutory purposes the term "members" may include employees who are prospective members.

**MINIMUM CONTRIBUTIONS** — Contributions payable to a personal pension scheme or to a free standing AVC scheme by the DSS in respect of a member who has elected to contract out. The contributions consist of a partial rebate of National Insurance contributions, together with the 2% incentive where applicable. The term could also be used in respect of any minimum amount which a member is required to contribute in order to be a member of an occupational or personal pension scheme, or in order to make additional voluntary contributions.

**MONEY PURCHASE** — The determination of an individual member's benefits by reference to contributions paid into the scheme in respect of that member, usually increased by an amount based on the investment return on those contributions.

**NET RELEVANT EARNINGS** — Earnings from self employment or non pensionable employment after deducting losses and certain business charges on income, used in determining the maximum contributions to a retirement annuity or personal pension scheme which qualify for tax relief. The maximum is currently 17.5% of net relevant earnings with higher contribution limits for older persons.

**NOMINATION** — The naming by a member of the person to whom he or she wishes any death benefit to be paid. The trust instrument will indicate whether this is binding on the trustees or merely for their consideration. In the latter case the term expression of wish is to be preferred.

**NON-CONTRIBUTORY SCHEME** — A pension scheme which does not require contributions from its active members. Not to be confused with a contributory scheme where contributions are suspended during a contribution holiday.

**OCCUPATIONAL PENSION SCHEME** — An arrangement organised by an employer or on behalf of a group of employers to provide pensions and/or other benefits for or in respect of one or more employees on leaving service or on death or retirement.

**OCCUPATIONAL PENSIONS BOARD (OPB)** — A statutory body set up under the Social Security Act 1973, with functions derived from that Act and the Social Security Pensions Act 1975. The Board is responsible for issuing contracting-out or appropriate scheme certificates for pension schemes which meet the statutory requirements, for supervising those schemes to ensure that guaranteed minimum pensions and protected rights are secure and for ensuring that equal treatment and preservation requirements are satisfied. The Board is required to report to the Secretary of State when he or she seeks their advice and to comment on draft regulations affecting occupational pension schemes.

**PENSIONABLE EARNINGS** — The earnings on which benefits and/or contributions are calculated. One or more elements of earnings (eg overtime) may be excluded, and/or there may be a state pension disregard.

**PENSIONABLE SERVICE** — The period of service which is taken into account in calculating pension benefit. The Social Security Act 1973 gives the term a statutory definition for the purposes of preservation, which also applies for the purposes of the revaluation and transfer payment requirements of the Social Security Pensions Act 1975.

**PERSONAL PENSION SCHEME** — Usually used to mean a scheme approved under Chapter IV of Part XIV of the Income and Corporation Taxes Act 1988, under which individuals who are self employed or in non pensionable employment make pension provision by means of insurance, unit trust or deposit account contracts. The Social Security Act 1986 uses a slightly different definition which excludes a scheme open only to the self employed but also includes a free standing AVC scheme.

**PRESERVATION** — The granting by a scheme of preserved benefits, in particular in accordance with minimum requirements specified by the Social Security Act 1973.

**PRESERVED BENEFITS** — Benefits arising on an individual ceasing to be an active member of a pension scheme, payable at a later date.

**PROTECTED RIGHTS** — The benefits under an appropriate personal pension scheme or a money purchase contracted-out scheme, deriving respectively from at least the minimum contributions or minimum payments, which are provided in a specified form as a necessary condition for contracting out. The term may also be used in a general sense to describe rights given to certain members on change of rules or change of pension scheme which are superior to those of a new entrant.

**QUALIFYING SERVICE** — The term defined in the Social Security Act

1973 denoting the service to be taken into account to entitle a member to short service benefit. The current condition is for at least two years' qualifying service.

**RELEVANT BENEFITS** — Retirement or death benefits which may be provided from an employer's approved scheme. If such benefits are provided under a retirement benefits scheme which is not an approved scheme, the cost or notional cost of them to the employer will be treated for tax purposes as remuneration paid to the employee.

**RETAINED BENEFITS** — Retirement or death benefits in respect of an employee deriving from an earlier period of employment or self employment. In some circumstances retained benefits must be included in the maximum approvable benefit.

**REVALUATION** — The application, particularly to preserved benefits, of indexation, escalation or the awarding of discretionary increases. The Social Security Pensions Act 1975 imposes revaluation in the calculation of guaranteed minimum pension and of preserved benefits other than guaranteed minimum pension. Revaluation is also an accounting term for the revision of the carrying value of an asset, usually having regard to its market value.

**SECTION 32 POLICY** — A term widely used to describe an insurance policy used for buy out purposes.

**SEGREGATED FUND** — An arrangement whereby the investments of a particular pension scheme are managed by an external investment manager independently of other funds under its control. Often used to indicate such an arrangement with an insurance company.

**SELF ADMINISTERED SCHEME** — A pension scheme where the assets are invested, other than wholly by payment of insurance premiums, by the trustees, an in-house manager or an external investment manager. Although on the face of it the term self administered should refer to the method of administering contributions and benefits, in practice the term has become solely related to the way in which the investments are managed.

**SELF INVESTMENT** — The investment of a scheme's assets in the business of the employer or that of an associated company, including loans made to the employer or associated company. The amounts of self investment requiring compulsory disclosure and reporting are laid down by the OPB and Disclosure Regulations. The SFO imposes restrictions on self investment by small self administered schemes.

**SERVICE** — A period of employment with one or more connected employers.

**SHORT SERVICE BENEFIT** — The benefit which must be provided for an early leaver under the preservation requirements of the Social Security Act 1973.

**TRANSFER PAYMENT** — A payment made from a pension scheme to another pension scheme, or to an insurance company to purchase a buy out policy, in lieu of benefits which have accrued to the member or members concerned, to enable the receiving arrangement to provide alternative benefits. The transfer payment may be made in accordance with the scheme rules or in exercise of a member's statutory rights under the Social Security Pensions Act 1975.

**TRANSFER VALUE** — A term commonly used to mean transfer payment.

**UPLIFTED 60ths** — Benefits in excess of $\frac{1}{60}$ of final remuneration for each year of service to the extent permitted by the SFO in an approved occupational pension scheme (other than a simplified scheme).

**UPPER BAND EARNINGS** — Earnings between the lower earnings limit and the upper earnings limit on which the additional component is calculated. Also used in the calculation of a guaranteed minimum pension.

**UPPER EARNINGS LIMIT** — The maximum amount of earnings (equal to approximately seven times the lower earnings limit) on which contributions are payable to the state scheme by employees.

**VESTED RIGHTS**
    (a) For active members, benefits to which they would unconditionally be entitled on leaving service;
    (b) for deferred pensioners, their preserved benefits;
    (c) for pensioners, pensions to which they are entitled;
including where appropriate the related benefits for spouses or other dependants.

**WAITING PERIOD** — A period of service specified in the rules which an employee must serve before being entitled to join the pension scheme or to receive a particular benefit. In some schemes the waiting period before being entitled to join may automatically count as pensionable service. Not to be confused with qualifying service.

# INDEX

Accounts .................................................... 61–2, 65
    contents ............................................... 61–2
Actuarial valuation and statement ....................... 62–3
Auditor's report ............................................... 62
Augmentation ................................................. 20–1
*Barber v Guardian Royal Exchange* ...................... 91–4
Benefit statements ............................................ 56–7
    annual ................................................... 66
Breach of trust ................................................ 89
Bulk transfers ................................................. 59
Buy-out policies .............................................. 136
Commutation ................................................. 18–19
Conflicts of interest ......................................... 13–14, 74
Contracting out .............................................. 122, 129–31
*Courage* case, the .......................................... 159–60
*Cowan v Scargill* ........................................... 34
*Davis v Richards & Wallington* ......................... 161
Death benefits ................................................ 20
Deferred pensioners ......................................... 13
Definitive trust deed ......................................... 4
Delegation ..................................................... 73
    rules of ................................................... 73–4
Disclosure of Information Regulations ................... 53–4
Discretionary pension increases .......................... 152
Early leaver statements ..................................... 58
Early retirement .............................................. 19
Equal treatment .............................................. 91–6
Exempt approved schemes ................................ 103
Family leave .................................................. 96
Finance Act 1989, restrictions ............................ 106
Financial Services Act 1986, the ......................... 43–6

Government Redundancy Fund ................................................ 15
Guaranteed minimum pensions ............................................ 129
    revaluation of ................................................ 129–30
*Hillsdown* case, the ............................................................. 159
*Icarus* case, the .................................................................. 160
*Imperial Tobacco Pension Fund* case, the ................................... 161–2
Information, disclosure ..................................................... 53–9
Interim trust deed ............................................................. 3–4
Investment
    definition of ............................................................. 45
    management ........................................................... 43–4
    rules ....................................................................... 33
Investment Management Regulatory Organisation (IMRO) ............ 43
Late entry ........................................................................ 18
Limited price indexation ................................................. 151–2
Maternity leave ................................................................. 96
Merger ........................................................................... 81
*Mettoy* case, the ............................................................. 160–1
National Insurance contributions .............................. 121, 129, 130
NUM pension scheme ......................................................... 34
Occupational Pensions Advisory Service, the .......................... 144
Occupational Pensions Board (OPB) .......................... 5, 88, 90, 119
Option statements .............................................................. 66
Pension schemes, rule changes ........................................... 21–2
Pensions
    increases ................................................................. 19
    occupational ......................................................... 122–3
    Ombudsman ...................................................... 55, 143
    State ................................................................... 121–2
Preserved benefits ......................................................... 133–4
Protected rights ............................................................ 130–1
Qualifying service ......................................................... 133–4
Refund of contributions ................................................... 133
Register of pension schemes ............................................ 143–4
Revaluation .................................................................... 134
Revenue limits .............................................................. 103–6
Scheme year .................................................................... 66
Securities and Investments Board (SIB) ................................. 43
Self-investment ........................................................ 35–6, 145
Signed and delivered ........................................................... 3

Social Security Act 1989, the ................................................. 96
Social Security Act 1990 .................................................. 35, 143
State Earnings Related Pension Scheme (SERPS) ... 121, 122, 123, 129, 130
Superannuation Funds Office ................................................. 7
Surpluses ........................................................ 88, 113–4, 119
Taxation ...................................................................... 103
Transfer credits ............................................................... 58
Transfer payments ..................................................... 17–18, 58
Transfers ................................................................... 135–6
    calculation of transfer value ................................... 135–6
    conditions for exercising the option .......................... 135
    right to ..................................................... 135
Treaty of Rome Article 119 ............................................... 91–2
Trust
    contract ...................................................... 1
    corporations .................................................. 6
    deed ......................................................... 4
    definition of ................................................. 1
    establishment of ............................................. 3
    Inland Revenue requirements ................................. 2
    reasons for .................................................. 2
Trustee Act 1925, the ............................................... 5, 73, 90
Trustee Investments Act 1961, the ....................................... 33
Trustees
    corporate .................................................... 89
    custodian ................................................... 6–7
    disagreements .............................................. 74–5
    discretionary powers of .................................... 17–22
    duties of .................................................. 13–15
    first ........................................................ 5
    independent ........................................ 7, 59, 144–5
    liability of ............................................... 89–90
    pensioneer ................................................... 7
    report ..................................................... 63–5
    resignation of .............................................. 5–6
    types of ..................................................... 6
Winding up the scheme ............................................ 59, 82, 160